120 Sample Write-Ups for Employee Performance Problems

A Manager's Guide to Documenting Reviews and Providing Appropriate Discipline

By: Dave Young

Table of Contents

Introduction

This book was written to help managers understand what is required of them when they are required to document employee performance problems and provide appropriate discipline. It is designed to help managers understand that the documentation they provide must clearly describe the employee's deficiencies and job performance problems, and why the disciplinary action is being taken.

This book provides managers with the tools needed to write clear, concise, and effective documentation on employee performance problems. It also provides many examples on how to write such documentation.

What are the benefits of reading this book?

Your company has a right to expect documentation that clearly documents job performance problems and employee deficiencies. This book will help you to do just that. You will learn how to create appropriate documentation for performance problems and discipline. You will be able to write clear, concise, and effective documentation that clearly describes the employee's deficiencies and job performance problems, and why disciplinary action is being taken. You will be able to develop appropriate documentation that is legally defensible.

Who should read this book?

This book was written for managers who are responsible for documenting performance problems and providing appropriate discipline. It is written for people who want to be compliant with their company's policies and procedures, as well as state and federal laws.

Without further delay, let's begin.

Chapter 1: Handling Performance Problems

Managers are expected to resolve performance problems. In many organizations, managers are expected to provide discipline when employees don't improve. This chapter describes the steps that should be taken and how to present documentation of performance problems in a way that will support the application of appropriate disciplinary action.

The process for documenting performance problems

1. List the performance issues and document them with a memo or e-mail to the employee (or employee's file) outlining what has happened and what needs to be improved. The memorandum should include a date, time, and a statement of when you will discuss the problem with the employee. Include your name and contact information on this memo or e-mail for reference later;
2. Provide feedback;
3. Discuss the problem in person with the employee; and,
4. Referral for counseling or other assistance (e.g., termination).

Let's take a look at these four steps in a little more detail with a few common scenarios that managers would encounter in the workplace.

Types of Performance Problems

There are many types of performance problems that can arise in the workplace. Some of the more common performance problems are below:

Continued Incompetence

The employee continues to exhibit incompetent performance and is not making any effort to improve his or her performance.

Lateness

The employee is habitually late for work. This may be due to poor time management, lack of planning, or a bad habit such as drinking too much coffee at home before leaving.

Absenteeism

The employee is habitually absent from work due to illness, family problems, substance abuse, or other problems.

Unauthorized Absence

The employee has had too many unauthorized absences. An absence is unauthorized if the workday or work week has not been officially designated as a paid time off (PTO) day.

Disrespectful Behavior

The employee is not showing respect to you, your fellow workers, or others in the workplace. This kind of behavior may include verbally insulting others, threatening others, and making physical threats to you or other employees.

Sexual Harassment

The employee is engaging in sexual harassment. Sexual harassment includes unwelcome sexual comments, requests for sexual favors, and physical contact of a sexual nature with another person in the workplace.

Refusal to Follow Directives

The employee refuses to follow your directives or orders given to him/her by you or another supervisor. Failure to carry out directives will result in discipline for insubordination. These directives may be given directly by you, an immediate supervisor, or a manager two levels above you who has authority over you and your employees. For example: You may be required to write up an employee who refuses direct orders from a manager at the next level of authority above you.

Disregard for Company Property

The employee has shown disrespect for equipment, supplies, and/or company property.

Cheating

The employee has cheated on work assignments or demonstrated a lack of integrity in completing work assignments. Cheating may include, but is not limited to plagiarizing reports, lying about the results of a project, or falsifying reports.

Lack of Teamwork

The employee is not participating in team activities and/or working cooperatively with others in the workplace. This kind of behavior may include being disruptive to other members of the team and engaging in activities that are detrimental to other members of the team. For example: Working too slowly which disrupts the work pace for fellow workers or refusing to participate in joint projects with other members of the team.

Incomplete Work

The employee is not completing assigned tasks and work assignments on time. This may be due to poor time management, lack of planning or procrastination. For example: An employee is supposed to complete a report by 5 PM each Friday but keeps putting it off until late into the evening hours each week before he or she finally completes it.

Poor Quality Work

An employee is producing work that is of unacceptable quality. This may be due to a lack of attention to detail, poor work habits or a lack of knowledge of the job duties. For example: An employee is writing a report about the performance of an employee who reports to him. The supervisor does not proofread his report before sending it to the manager above him for approval. The manager reads the report and determines that it is poorly written and filled with spelling and grammatical errors. The manager reprimands the supervisor for not proofreading his own report before sending it for review by his manager.

Defiance

The employee has defied your authority and/or disobeyed your direct orders or directives. Disobedience may also include insubordination such as refusing to follow directives given by other supervisors with authority over you or refusing direct orders from you, an immediate supervisor, or a manager two levels above you who has authority over you and your employees. For example: You are asked by your immediate supervisor if you will take on an additional task during lunch hours each week in addition to completing your regular assignments during your regular work hours each day. Upon receiving this request, you refuse direct orders from both your immediate supervisor and the manager two levels above you who has authority over you.

Inappropriate Behavior

The employee is behaving inappropriately in the workplace. This kind of behavior may include, but is not limited to cursing, harassing, threatening, touching other employees in a sexual manner, and engaging in inappropriate conversations at work. For example: An employee shouts swear words at another worker. The swearing worker then turns his attention toward you and shouts an obscene gesture toward you as well. You note this incident in your personal notes and plan to address it with the employee who behaved inappropriately.

Abandoning Work

The employee has abandoned his or her assigned tasks to complete another type of job for which he or she has no authorization from a supervisor to do so. For example: An employee working in the shipping department quits working on packing crates during normal work hours to work on a pre-approved project for another department within the company, but without authorization from an immediate supervisor or manager two levels above you who has authority over you and your employees to do so.

The above list is not all inclusive of all the types of performance problems that can occur in your workplace. However, it does include some of the more common performance problems that managers encounter when dealing with their employees. Once you have identified what type of performance problems you are dealing with, you should then decide which method of discipline will best address the problem.

Most managers understand the importance of conducting disciplinary conferences with employees who have violated rules, regulations, policies, etc., but many managers are not aware of the legal considerations involved in conducting effective disciplinary conferences with their employees. A disciplinary conference is a meeting with an employee to discuss the reasons for discipline and to inform the employee of the action that will be taken.

Managers should be aware that any disciplinary action that they take may result in a lawsuit being filed by an aggrieved employee. What follows are some legal considerations managers need to know about their disciplinary practices:

1. Employers have a right to discipline employees for misconduct or violations of company rules, but employers must also pay attention to how and when they discipline employees. Disciplinary actions taken by employers can lead to successful lawsuits if not done properly.

2. Employers can discipline employees for any type of misconduct or rule violation, but they cannot discipline employees in a manner that is not related to the misconduct.

3. The punishment must fit the misconduct. If an employee is guilty of stealing from the company, for example, he or she should be warned first, and then fired if the theft continues. A manager cannot fire an employee for stealing with sufficient proof to back their claims.

4. Disciplinary action must be taken immediately - there are no exceptions to this rule because it is still considered immediate even if it takes place during the next shift after the misconduct occurred. *Note:* Sometimes a manager may want to have another person present during a disciplinary action to make sure that both parties are acting in good faith and not trying to pull one over on each other.

7

5. A manager can never discipline an employee for misconduct for things that the employee has never indulged in. For example, if an employee was accused of being late for work or misbehaving at work but was proved to be false, it could spoil the reputation of the firm and concerned managers.

6. Managers should not discipline employees on their breaks or lunch hours if they do not have another person present to witness the disciplinary action and take notes of what was said during the conference - this is important in case there is a lawsuit filed by an aggrieved employee and a court asks to see notes taken during the disciplinary conference. Ideally, managers should avoid disciplining an employee off site - even if they are going out for lunch together or running errands as it can be construed as being unfair to an employee.

7. A manager must never treat one employee differently than another employee who has committed similar misconduct - this is called disparate treatment and can lead to successful lawsuits by aggrieved employees against their employers. Such forms of treatment will affect the moral of the employees and create a feeling of hatred in the workplace.

These are the basic legal concerns that should be addressed by managers who are conducting disciplinary conferences with their employees. The more attention a manager pays to these legal considerations, the less likely he/she is to run into problems with lawsuits.

Methods of Discipline in the Workplace

A method of discipline is defined as any written or verbal statement used by an employer to express its disapproval about an employee's job performance (such as a reprimand, complaint, warning, or criticism). As a manager, you have been trained in the "What" and "Why" of disciplining your employees. You know what method of discipline to use and why you should use it. You also know how to document your employee's performance problems and provide appropriate discipline. There is still one step that can make your work easier -the "How".

The "How" is the method of discipline you will use to correct your employee's performance problem. The method of discipline will vary depending on the type of performance problem you are addressing.

As a manager, you may find yourself using any number of methods to correct an employee's performance problems. Some methods include verbal counseling, written warnings, suspensions, demotions, terminations, and layoffs. Each method has its advantages and disadvantages depending on the type of problem being corrected as well as the needs or desires of both the employer and employee.

The first step in deciding which method to use is determining what type of performance problem you are correcting by using some form of discipline. Once you have identified the type or types of problems you are correcting, the next step is to decide which method of discipline will best address the problem.

Verbal Counseling

Verbal counseling is usually used to correct minor performance problems on the job. It is a short discussion with the employee about a specific performance problem. An example of verbal counseling might be telling an employee that there are parts of their job they are doing well but there are also parts of the job they need to improve on. This type of counseling session should not take more than 10 or 15 minutes. If you find yourself spending more time with an employee discussing a problem, it might be better to get them involved in a performance improvement plan or write them up using a written warning instead. Additionally, the employer or manager can make permanent records of the anecdotal counselling notes as a form of reference. In the event of future discrepancies, they could serve as proof and appropriate action can be taken.

Advantages

Verbal counseling is simple and relatively informal, so it does not have to be documented in writing like other methods do. Since verbal counseling is informal, you can warn an employee about their problems without making them feel as if they are being reprimanded for poor work habits or inadequate work quality.

Disadvantages

As verbal counseling is so simple and informal, there is a greater chance that the employee will not understand why you are counseling them. This makes it more difficult to address the problem in an effective manner. You must also remember that when you apologize for something, you end up making an admission of guilt. For example, if you point out an employee's mistakes, you can emphasize the fact that advice is given in an effort to avoid recurring mistakes and to improve the employee's quality of work instead of apologizing. Additionally, verbal counseling also serves as an anecdotal record of your counseling sessions with an employee. Finally, because verbal counseling is so brief and informal, there is a greater chance that employees will not take your concerns about their performance or problems on the job as important and not change the behavior.

Written Warnings

Written warnings are used for correcting more serious performance problems on the job. An example of a written warning might be telling an employee that they are performing poorly on the job and need to improve their performance or face termination from their job within a certain period of time. Written warnings can be issued by both management and non-management employees, but they have certain requirements that must be followed by all managers. You will have to document your discussions with the employee if they dispute the allegations made against them. It is also important that you give your employees a copy of their written warning so they know what their problems are and how they can correct them quickly before termination becomes a possibility.

Advantages

Written warnings can be used to correct major performance problems. Since they are documented in writing, they allow you to create a record of your counseling sessions with an employee. They can also be used to educate the employees about the performance problem and give them time to correct it before you take more serious action. Finally, since written warnings are given in writing, they require the employee's signature. This gives you proof that the employee was informed of their poor work habits or inadequate work quality.

Disadvantages

You must remember that when you write a warning letter for poor performance or inadequate job skills, you are only creating a record of what is wrong with your employee's performance or employment history. Since it is possible for employees to contest documentation about their poor performance or inadequate job skills, written warnings may not be sufficient evidence if legal action results from termination of employment. Finally, you need to remember that written warnings are not effective for correcting all types of performance problems.

Suspensions

Suspensions are used to correct employee performance problems that can lead to termination or other disciplinary actions. An example of a suspension is informing an employee that they have been temporarily suspended from work owing to reasons such as misconduct in the workplace or disputes with co-workers. Suspensions can be either paid or unpaid depending on the situation. They are usually given for a set period of time and then the employee is allowed to return to work. Because suspensions can result in termination, they should only be used for serious problems such as insubordination or drug abuse. It is also important that you inform your employee's supervisor about the suspension, so they are aware of what is happening and what action needs to be taken to correct it when your employee returns from suspension.

Advantages

Suspensions give you time to make sure your employees understand why they have been suspended and how they can take adequate action to correct their mistakes. Since suspensions greatly influence the final outcome, you can decide whether you should terminate the employee or give them another chance to make amends. Finally, you can utilize suspensions to highlight the seriousness of the situation. As it is a form of disciplinary action, it allows employers to enforce their strict policies against disruptive employees who do not heed to repeated warnings.

Disadvantages

Suspensions are used in situations where employees have shown a lack of respect for management or the company's policies and procedures. The entire process of suspension must include a fair reason to actually suspend an employee. Without a valid reason, it would be classified under unfair labor practices, which would result in the employer spending more money on employee compensation according to the CCMA. It is also important to remember that since suspensions can lead to termination, they should only be used if all other previous methods have failed. In most cases, a suspended employee is entitled to pay unless if conflicts with their contractual rights. If an employee is suspended, someone else has to shoulder the responsibilities of the workload. This results in additional expenses to allocate other employees to complete the pending tasks, which adversely affects the productivity of the workplace.

Demotions are used when an employee has shown incompetence on his current job. The demotion is simply a transfer to a job where the employee has shown competence. If you demote an employee, you are not punishing them, you are simply moving them to a job where they can perform adequately. The advantages and disadvantages of demotions are:

Advantages

Employees who have been demoted can earn their way back into the position they lost if their performance improves. If a demotion is accompanied by training to improve their job skills, it gives your company and the employee an opportunity to see if that employee has the ability and desire to learn new skills which will allow them to return to their old position or advance within your company. Demoting an employee allows you time to evaluate whether this employee can improve their work performance before terminating their employment. Additionally, demotions involve a lower degree of risk. Reduced pay from demotion of employees also can help the firm save additional expenses.

Disadvantages

Demoting employees does not mean that they will continue performing adequately, even on the new job. When employees are moved from one position or department in a company to another, they are often bitter over the demotion and won't do their best on their new job. Sometimes, demoted employees may choose to quit their job instead of improving themselves. Also, unfair demotions could result in lawsuits, which could result in significant damage to the firm.

Terminations are used when an employee's performance is so poor that it would be impossible to improve their job skills or work habits to adequately perform their job. You can terminate an employee for numerous reasons, including insubordination, substance abuse, conflicts with other employees, and poor attendance. Most employers require terminated employees to sign a release form stating that they will not sue the company for wrongful termination before paying them their final paycheck or benefits. However, you should consult your legal counsel before signing this form, because it may limit the company's ability to defend itself if a lawsuit is filed against it. While terminations are usually handled by Human Resources, they are still your responsibility, because you hired the employee, and you are responsible for terminating them. The advantages and disadvantages of terminations are:

Advantages

The threat of termination is the most direct way of correcting poor performance since you are giving the employee an ultimatum - either improve your job performance or get terminated. Terminations allow you to make sure that everyone else in your department knows that poor job performance will not be tolerated, which encourages employees to constantly improve themselves and work towards the progress of the firm.

Disadvantages

If the termination is handled poorly it could lead to a lawsuit against your company; therefore, it is important that you document every step in the process carefully along with what led up to your decision to terminate this employee. If you do not handle the termination properly, the employee could claim that you have discriminated against them based on age, gender, race or disability. Poorly handled terminations could also lead to trouble with other employees who might feel that they were treated unfairly Finally, if you decide to terminate multiple employees, it could result in an unstable workplace with overworked employees, which could affect company morale.

As a manager, it is important that you understand all methods of discipline you can use when correcting employee performance problems, so that you can choose the method that will give your employees the most opportunity to improve their job skills and work habits. Let's now get into the legal considerations of taking such disciplinary actions.

Legal Considerations

It is always best to document your employee's performance problems. This usually means that you must put the employee on a Performance Improvement Plan (PIP). Although it is not good for business, in some cases it may be necessary to terminate the employee. The termination of an employee has significant legal implications for both the employer and the employee. Failure to follow proper written procedures may result in:

Unlawful termination of an employee

A written procedure reinforcing your right to terminate an employee for just cause will allow you to protect yourself from wrongful termination suits or claims by disgruntled employees.

Breach of contract

A PIP with specific goals and time frames that are not met could be held to be a breach of contract.

Damages

If you fail to follow proper procedures, you might have to pay damages such as back wages and front wages (up-front damages), punitive damages, liquidated damages (double damages), interest on damages, court costs, attorney fees and expert witness fees.

Time off from work

If your company does not have a policy in place under which employees can take time off from work, you may find yourself exposed if an employee files suit against you for unpaid leave time or unpaid vacation time.

How do you avoid these problems?

Documentation is the key to avoiding these problems. As a manager, you must possess documentation of every business occurrences such as employment contracts, performance appraisal documents, and relevant statutory documents. In the event of any disputes, a comprehensive record of all verbal and non-verbal legal documents must be produced.

In particular, what was said or done by the employee, what you said or did, and the result of the discussion should be recorded. With these events and conversations, you will be able to defend yourself against any charges brought against you by an employee. Even if no charges are made against you, the written record that you have kept will be valuable in the case of future legal action. You must also follow proper procedures with regard to your method of discipline in the workplace to protect yourself from legal action taken by employees. The following are some methods of discipline that are commonly used in most businesses:

Oral Communication

This involves discussing with an employee about his or her performance problems without putting it in writing first. This is usually only done during the initial stage when there is little doubt about the problem and its severity.

Formal Written Acknowledgement

This method of discipline is used when there is doubt regarding the problem or the severity of it. It also allows you to follow up on the verbal communication with a permanent record of the discussions involved.

Written Reprimand

This is used when there is substantial doubt about the problem or the severity of it. This method of discipline is usually a last resort if other methods of discipline have not worked, and you want to formally warn the employee that he or she could be terminated if he/she does not improve his/her performance.

What Can You Do?

Managers who wish to avoid all these potential problems must maintain clear records of their dealings with employees. In addition, they must follow proper procedures as outlined in this guide when dealing with employee performance problems and complaints. They must also document the reasons for the termination of an employee. All managers should be aware of the legal implications of their actions and how to avoid potential problems.

Notification of Disciplinary Action

This section is the first part of the write-up that will show a manager's approach to discipline. The Notification of Disciplinary Action section is one that any manager needs to put some time and thought into writing. It sets the tone for all subsequent sections in the write-up, and it is the first introduction to a problem employee by their new supervisor. The following are some points that should be considered when drafting this section:

Provide sufficient detail in this section to allow for an understanding of what happened, why disciplinary action was taken, what rules were violated and what corrective action will be taken. This is not meant to be an exhaustive list of events, but rather a summary of relevant events.

Try to stick as closely as possible to facts and avoid including opinions or comments about the actions of the employee. This is not an appropriate place for a manager's opinion about someone's character, personality, or their work habits. This can come across as unwarranted personal criticism by the employer if it comes from a non-supervisory employee, and it can make the employer subject to legal scrutiny if it's done by a supervisor.

Open with a statement that covers the main facts of the situation, such as "Your employment record shows that you have violated Company X's Employee Code of Conduct in an incident on XXX-XX-XXXX."

Include details of what happened providing relevant dates and times, names of persons involved, names of witnesses, and any other relevant information such as what was said and/or seen. Try to provide a complete picture of what occurred. This is not the time to be vague or incomplete, and this is not a place for opinions about either side. Stick to facts.

Since this is intended as part of a legal document, include sufficient detail so that no one could say they were misled or did not know enough about the situation to provide informed consent to any decision or action taken against them. Even though most employers will consider this section confidential, there are still legal requirements for employers to ensure workers are fully informed before taking action against them. This means there must be sufficient detail provided, so there is no reasonable belief that any worker could feel misled due to their actions taking disciplinary action against them.

State clearly that this is a violation of the Company X Employee Code of Conduct and explicitly identify the specific rule(s) that have been violated. For example, "You have violated section 2-6 of the Company X Employee Code of Conduct," or "You have violated rule 16a in the Company X Employee Handbook." Do not assume that they will know which rule they have broken or why it is a rule, so state clearly that this is a violation of the Company X Employee Code of Conduct.

If there are multiple incidents to be addressed in this write-up, then make sure to clearly state which incident(s) are being addressed, and then provide sufficient detail for each one separately. This will allow for each incident to stand on its own without making any assumption as to what actions occurred in any other incidents that may be described separately later in the write-up.

Only after including all relevant details about one or more violations should you then provide any corrective action to take against them, such as stripping them of some privileges, placing them on probation, demoting them, transferring them to another position, terminating their employment, etc. You should also include details about how they will be made aware of any changes to their employment status, such as if they will be placed on leave or transferred to a different position.

You should provide details on how each corrective action will be implemented and when those actions will occur. For example, "You are hereby placed on probation for the next 30 days. If there are no further incidents during this time, you will return to your normal status with Company X."

It is also important to include details on any other actions that may be taken as a result of this incident, including disciplinary action against other employees involved in the incident in addition to the employee being written up.

If it is determined that an employee has violated a company policy more than once, then make sure you clearly state this fact, and then explain why you have not taken stronger disciplinary action against them up to this point.

Remember that you should not leave any room for anyone to misunderstand or misinterpret the proceeding of the situation.

Sufficient evidence must be provided to the employee to allow them to know the reaction reason for receiving adequate disciplinary action. Furthermore, this will remove the feeling of uncertainty among other employees and will ensure that your company conducts a fair process.

Example:

> Employee: John Doe, Employee ID: xxx-xx-XXXX
>
> Company X's Employee Code of Conduct states: "All employees are expected to conduct themselves appropriately and professionally at all times and in all locations. All employees are expected to work toward the Company X mission statement and strive to achieve its goals by meeting or exceeding the Company's standards for customer service while maintaining high levels of performance as demonstrated by their overall job performance scores."
>
> On XX-XX-20XX, John Doe was observed arriving at work at XX: XX am with a noticeable odor of alcohol coming from his breath while being visibly intoxicated. He was also overheard making inappropriate comments about other employees at work during this time period while being visibly intoxicated. This is a violation of both rule 2-6 "Attendance, Punctuality, and Other Issues Related to Work Performance" and rule 7-5 "Use of Alcoholic Beverages and Other Substances."
>
> Company X has previously documented prior incidents in which John Doe violated the Company X Employee Code of Conduct in instances on XX-XX-20XX, XX-XX-20XX, XX-XX-20XX, and XX-XX-20XX. In each of these incidents it was documented that John Doe arrived at work smelling strongly of alcohol while being visibly intoxicated. It was also documented that on these dates he made inappropriate comments to other employees at work while being visibly intoxicated.

In each of these instances, John Doe was counseled about his actions on the previous occasion(s) by his supervisor and warned that any further violations would result in more severe disciplinary action being taken.

Since that time there have been no further incidents of John Doe arriving to work intoxicated at work or making inappropriate comments to other employees while being visibly intoxicated.

As a result of previous incidents, this is now considered a second level violation which will be addressed with immediate termination of his employment with Company X. John Doe's employment with Company X will be terminated effective immediately and he will receive wages through XX-XX-20XX for any hours worked through that date at which point he will receive no further payment. His final paycheck will be payable on or before XX-XX-20XX.

John Doe will also be required to complete an approved alcohol abuse rehabilitation program before he can return to employment with Company X if he wishes to do so in the future. If he does not complete the rehabilitation program or returns to work with Company X while still in possession of alcohol, then he will be terminated immediately upon discovery.

Company X will inform John Doe that he is being placed on probation for the next 30 days. If there are no further incidents during this time, he will return to his normal status with the company. If there are any further incidents during this time, then further disciplinary action will be taken against him including termination of his employment with Company X.

John Doe is currently employed as a Customer Service Representative at Company X and his current hourly wage rate is $X / hour. His current work schedule consists of working XX hours per week (X days per week) and he has been employed by Company X since XX-XX-20XX until today's date, when it was determined that he violated the Employee Code of Conduct and was terminated effective immediately. He has worked at Company X for a total of YY years and ZZ months and has worked XXX hours total up to this point in time.

A copy of this write-up will be provided to John Doe as a part of the disciplinary action being taken against him. He will also be informed that he has the right to appeal this decision as per the Company X Employee Code of Conduct. Any appeal that he files will be reviewed by the Human Resources Director and a decision will be made whether or not to uphold, overturn, or modify the disciplinary action taken against him.

If John Doe does not appeal this decision, then one copy of this write-up will be placed in his personnel file along with all other documentation relating to his employment with Company X. Another copy of this write-up will also be placed in John Doe's personnel file along with all other documentation relating to his employment with Company X should he decide to withdraw his appeal. If John Doe decides to withdraw his appeal, then a copy of this write-up, along with all other documentation relating to his employment at Company X, will remain in his personnel file for a period of YY years and ZZ months from today's date after which it will be removed from his file and destroyed permanently.

Sincerely,

[Appropriate Signature Authority]

Enclosure:

I have received a copy and am aware of the contents of the foregoing letter.

Employee Signature
_____ Date _____

Employee Confrontation

Employees become angry and their emotions can get the best of them. There is no denying that confrontations between employees can lead to verbal and physical abuse They are sometimes upset because they do not think their boss is doing a good job, or they may feel that they are being treated unfairly. Confrontations between two or more employees can also lead to violence and the need for intervention from management or security officers. In these situations, the manager needs to make it clear that any employee who acts out violently will be disciplined severely. The manager should call in security and never try to settle such situations on his or her own - even if he or she is physically bigger than the aggressor.

Management has a right to protect itself by having other employees restrain an individual who has been violent with management or another employee. Security officers should be called if there is no other staff member able to help with restraining an individual under attack by another employee.

Employee Common Rebuttal

This section will discuss the common reasons that employees give for challenging their disciplinary action. This is simply to ensure that the manager has the right policies and procedures in place to deal with them.

Employee Reason #1

"*I wasn't given a chance to tell my side of the story.*"

Remedy

Have a clear written procedure for disciplinary action that provides for the employee's right to be heard. Make sure your managers comply with the procedures in every case.

Employee Reason #2

"*I was not given a warning before I was fired.*"

Remedy

Have a clear written policy that provides for progressive discipline before termination or other serious disciplinary actions, such as suspension. Make sure your managers comply with the policies in every case. Make sure managers document each step along the way and keep good records of conversations with employees about their performance problems. Have managers meet with these employees at least once every month to review performance problems and discuss possible solutions.

If problems continue, have your managers begin documenting performance issues and implement disciplinary actions, including suspensions and terminations. Document all meetings, conversations, and written warnings in an employee's file before any disciplinary action is taken. This will show that you were following proper procedures before you terminate an employee, and will help you defend yourself from potential legal challenges by disgruntled former employees who feel they were treated unfairly or not given a fair chance to improve their performance.

"I was fired for discriminatory reasons."

Remedy

Ensure that managers follow all your company's policies and procedures to avoid discrimination in the workplace and comply accordingly. Make sure managers are aware of the need for special care in dealing with employees who may be older than 40, who are disabled or who may belong to a racial or ethnic minority group.

Carefully document any disciplinary actions taken and be sure employees understand which types of performance will not be tolerated and that they will face disciplinary action if they do not improve their performance. Document all complaints, investigations, and disciplinary actions regarding alleged discrimination. A thorough and fair review process is the best way to protect yourself from discrimination claims by disgruntled former employees. If you have a formal grievance procedure in place, make sure your managers comply with it accordingly.

Employee Reason #4

"My manager was mean to me when he disciplined me." (or) "He treated me unfairly because he was angry at me for some reason." (or) "He let other employees off easy when they did the same thing I did, even though I was the only one he disciplined over it." (or) "The manager is always picking on me for no reason at all."

Remedy

Ensure that managers who conduct disciplinary actions are aware of the importance of doing so in a professional and respectful manner. Make sure managers understand their obligation to treat all employees equally and know how to respond appropriately if they feel the need to discipline an employee for poor performance. Make sure your managers have a clear understanding of the reasons for your company's discipline policies and procedures. If your company has a formal grievance procedure, make sure that your managers comply with it accordingly.

Employee Reason #5

"My manager didn't give me a chance to improve my performance before he fired me."

Remedy

Always have a clear procedure for conducting disciplinary actions that provides for the employee's right to know about any performance problems and to be given an opportunity to improve before any disciplinary action is taken. Make sure managers understand the procedures in every case. If you have a formal grievance procedure in place, make sure your managers comply with it accordingly. Make sure your managers implement progressive discipline in every case where appropriate, and that they meet with employees at least once every month during the performance improvement process.

Employee Reason #6

"My manager was unfair when he wrote me up or disciplined me." (or) "He gave me a false warning about my performance when there was nothing wrong with it." (or) "He never gave me a chance to improve my performance."

Remedy

Have the employee sign a statement in which he or she acknowledges that the warning was given, that the warning has been explained and that it was not a disciplinary action, but simply a "warning."

"My manager gave me a disciplinary action when I was off work or out sick." (or) "He gave me a letter of reprimand when I wasn't even at work that day." (or) "He gave me a written warning when he knew I was on vacation." (or) "I had to take time off work to attend an informal meeting with my manager, and then I was fired for it."

Remedy

This is a problem that arises in an organization where managers are required to write-up or discipline employees, although they were not present for the infraction. It is easier said than done, but you must train your managers not to discipline employees in their absence, unless it is an emergency situation, which is extremely rare. Even if it was an emergency situation, you still have a problem in that there was no one present at the time of the event who could have witnessed or documented what happened. If your organizational policy requires that a manager write up or discipline an employee who is not present, then you need your managers to have the presence of mind to document that they were not able to talk with the employee and why this was the case.

"My manager gave me a disciplinary action when I was out sick for more than three days." (or) "I told my manager that I would be out for three days, but he did not give me a chance to explain why I needed more time off." (or) "He gave me a written warning after he found out that I had taken time off without permission." (or) "My manager fired me when she knew that I was going on vacation and she knew it was approved in advance."

Remedy

The best remedy for avoiding this problem is to have your managers follow some type of discipline policy, which states how much notice is required before taking some type of action against an employee who will be absent from work for an extended period of time. If there is no such policy in your company, then you need to make sure that your managers understand the legal implications and set of procedures they should follow to make sure that the employee is given ample opportunity to explain his or her absence for the extended period of time.

Now that we have covered the basics of handling performance issues for managers, let's get into specific scenarios that requires you to write a write-up for common employee performance problems in the following chapters.

Chapter 2: Probation Employee Performance

Of all the employee performance problems, probationary employees are the most common. Probationary employees are employees who work for a specific period of time without benefits.

Performance Standard

The employee will meet the terms of his/her probationary period. The employee will receive a review with a Probationary Review Checklist to ensure that he/she is meeting the probationary requirements as established by the Company. The review must be conducted on a regular basis as specified by the company policies during the probationary period.

Probationary Employee Performance Problems

Employees are placed on probation for a variety of reasons, but most often it is because they have not met expectations during their initial employment review period. Sometimes an employee's performance problem can be corrected by additional training or coaching, but this is not always possible. If an employee's performance does not improve after he/she has been given adequate opportunity to improve his/her performance, or if the situation is so serious that it cannot be resolved through training or coaching, then disciplinary action may be warranted.

Probationary employee performance problems are not always as clear as the other employee performance problems. It is often difficult to determine when probationary employees have reached the point where they should be terminated because their performance is not improving, or because they are unable to meet minimum job requirements. As a manager, you will need to use your best judgment and the information provided in this guide when determining if a probationary employee needs corrective action at any particular time.

We will share various write-ups for probationary employee performance problems:

1. Extending the Length of Probation

After an employee has been on probation for a specific period of time, it may become clear that the employee is not meeting expectations and that he/she may need to be terminated. It is not necessary to wait until the end of the probationary period before beginning corrective action. If, after a probationary period has ended, it becomes clear that an employee's performance problems have persisted, then you should begin corrective action by providing the employee with verbal warnings or written warnings, as appropriate.

For each probationary employee whose issues have not been corrected, you should write a probationary write-up similar to the provided templates. It is important that you document in writing the steps you have taken to correct the employee's problem so that it can be documented in case there is a subsequent dispute over whether you have fulfilled your obligation to provide feedback and coaching or not. Use the following template for extending the length of time on probation:

Date

Employee Name

(Problem Relevance) - Probationary Performance Problem
(Problem Cause) -The cause of the employee's problem performance is identified to be a lack of skills, especially in

programming. An employee's performance has not met the minimum standards of acceptable performance for this job.

(Problem Analysis) - The employee has been provided with training, coaching, and assistance to correct his/her problem.

(Action Taken) - I have attempted to correct the employee's problem performance by providing feedback and coaching and also gave him/her multiple chances to improve his/her performance by providing additional training, but it has not improved.

(Action Required) -The employee is expected to improve his/her performance by _____, or he/she will be terminated.

(Solution) - I will be terminating the employment relationship unless there is significant improvement in his/her performance within _____ days. The employee's probationary period will be extended for _____ days.

Approved By: Date

Manager Signature and Title

2. Terminating a Probationary Employee

If an employee's performance does not improve after his/her probationary period has ended, then you should terminate the employment relationship. Keep in mind that if a probationary employee is terminated for poor job performance, then his/her job offer can't be revoked in the future as they no longer work for the particular company. It is also difficult to re-employ the same employee. Use the following template for terminating a probationary employee:

Date

Employee Name

(Problem Relevance) - Termination of Probationary Employee.
(Problem Cause) - The cause of the employee's problem performance is found to be a lack of motivation in fulfilling his/her goals. The employee's probationary period has deemed the performance to not meet the minimum standards of acceptable performance.
(Problem Analysis) - The employee has been provided with training, coaching, and assistance to correct his/her problem.
(Action Taken) I have attempted to correct the employee's problem performance by providing feedback and coaching. In addition, I have given him/her multiple chances to improve his/her performance by providing additional training, but it has not improved.
(Solution) - I will be terminating the employment relationship unless there is significant improvement in his/her performance within _____ days.

Approved By: Date

Manager Signature and Title

3. Probationary Employee Who Was Late for Work

If a probationary employee constantly arrives late for work, then you should write a probationary employee tardiness notification. If the probationary employee remains late for work, then you should terminate the employment relationship. Use the following template for probationary employees who are late for work:

Date

Employee Name

(Problem Relevance) - Probationary Employee Tardiness.
(Problem Cause) - The cause of the employee's tardiness is discovered to be a lack of punctuality. The employee has been consistently late for work on a regular basis.
(Problem Analysis) - The employee has been provided with training, coaching, and assistance to correct his/her problem.
(Action Taken) - I have attempted to correct the employee's tardiness by providing feedback and coaching. I have given him/her multiple chances to improve his/her performance by providing additional training, but it has no improvement. Therefore, I will be terminating the employment relationship unless there is significant improvement in his/her performance within _____ days.
(Solution) - The employment relationship is being terminated immediately because there is no longer a need for this position at this time. However, if asked to return to work in the future, it will be as a probationary employee. If he/she is terminated again, it will be for good cause, which can make it difficult to re-employ him/her.

Approved By: Date

Manager Signature and Title

4. Probationary Employee Who Failed to Follow Instructions

If a probationary employee continually fails to follow instructions or perform assigned duties, then you should write a probationary employee failure to follow instructions notification. If the probationary employee continues to exhibit this behavior, then you should terminate the employment relationship. Use the following template for probationary employee who failed to follow instructions:

Date

Employee Name

(Problem Relevance) - Probationary Employee Failure to Follow Instructions.

(Problem Cause) - The cause of the employee's failure to follow instructions is found to be disobedience and conflicting with company guidelines. The employee has been repeatedly instructed on how to perform his/her duties but has continued to fail to follow instructions.

(Problem Analysis) - In an attempt to improve his/her performance, the employee has been provided with training, coaching, and assistance to correct his/her problem.

(Action Taken) - I have attempted to correct the employee's failure to follow instructions by proper coaching. I have given him/her multiple chances to improve his/her performance by providing additional training. Therefore, I will be terminating the employment relationship unless there is significant improvement in his/her performance within _____ days.

(Solution) - The employment relationship is being terminated immediately because he/she is deemed not fit for the role currently. However, if asked to return to work in the future, it will be as a probationary employee. If he/she is terminated again, it will be for good cause, which can make it difficult to re-employ him/her.

Approved By: Date

Manager Signature and Title

Chapter 3: Employee Policy Infringements

This chapter discusses the various policy violations that employees can commit. It describes how to handle each type of policy violation and provides an example of a write-up for each. There are many different types of policy violations that employees can commit. We will focus on the serious violations that can lead to termination. Many of the write-ups will be for violations that result in termination, but there are some that do not and others for which it is necessary to start with a more serious write-up.

Every company has a set of policies that it expects employees to follow. Employees are expected to read and understand these policies. If they are unsure, they can request for further information from the concerned authorities to clarify any doubts. In addition, employees are expected to know what types of behavior are prohibited by the policies and what type of behavior is permitted. The policies should address all possible situations where an employee might commit a policy violation and state specifically what employees can do or cannot do in these situations. Your company may have several different policies covering several different areas of your business, such as safety, harassment, or theft prevention. The goal is to make sure that all employees comply with the policy and understand the consequences if they do not comply.

To ensure compliance with your company's policies, you should periodically remind your employees about them and make sure they are aware of any changes that you have made over time or any recent additions/modifications made by other managers. Postings on bulletin boards, company websites, and email reminders can help you accomplish this.

If an employee violates a policy, it is often useful to document what happened and how the employee violated the policy. This is particularly important when the violation is serious enough that the employee may be terminated or when there is a pattern of violations by the employee. The types of documentation that you should consider are described below. Note that many of these documents will use terms such as "willful" or "intentional" to describe certain types of violations. Remember that policies are not meant to focus on minor, unintentional violations, but rather on situations where employees intentionally violate a policy or act in a manner that they know would violate a policy.

The documentation that you create should focus on how the employee violated the policy and why he violated it. In some cases, you may also want to include information about what led up to the violation or what consequences resulted from it. This last part may not be necessary if you have a particularly serious violation or serious consequences and will focus on those in your write-up and/or conversation with the employee.

Remember that part of your job as a manager is to make sure that employees are aware of and follow the policies. It is not acceptable for you to overlook policy violations just because they are minor or unintentional. It is also not acceptable for you to overlook a pattern of minor or unintentional violations by an employee because you know that he has been violating a policy repeatedly and has never seriously considered the consequences of his actions. You may want to consider whether to implement more frequent inspections of work areas to help prevent violations. Let's take a look at some of the more common and serious policy violations that can result in termination.

5. Alcohol in the Workplace

Alcohol in the workplace is a serious problem in many companies. It is also one of the most common policy infractions that result in termination. Most employers prevent alcohol from being consumed anywhere on their premises, but there are some who allow employees to drink alcohol at lunch or after work, either at an employee lounge or in their own offices. Some employers allow employees who are on medication to take it with an alcoholic beverage. No matter what your policy is regarding alcohol in the workplace, it must be consistently applied to all employees and enforced appropriately. Use the following template for alcohol in the workplace:

Date

Employee Name

(Problem Relevance) - Employee Consumption of Alcohol in the Workplace.
(Problem Cause) - The cause of the employee's alcohol consumption is deemed to be addiction to liquor.
(Problem Analysis) - The employee was observed drinking alcohol at his/her desk during lunch.
(Action Taken) - I have advised the employee that it is our policy to prohibit employees from consuming alcohol at any time on our premises.
(Solution) - The employee will be required to attend a (state type of meeting or training session, such as a counseling or training session).

Approved By: Date

Manager Signature and Title

6. Workplace Violence

It is important to prevent workplace violence because it can lead to injuries and deaths. Workplace violence can take many forms, including threats, physical harm, and harassment. It can occur between employees or between an employee and a customer. If you have a policy that prohibits violence against anyone at work, then you must enforce it consistently when someone violates it. Use the following template for workplace violence:

Date

Employee Name

(Problem Relevance) - Workplace Violence.
(Problem Cause) - The employee has exhibited behaviors that violate our policy prohibiting workplace violence.
(Problem Analysis) - The employee was observed (state act or behavior) towards a coworker on _____ occasions.
(Action Taken) - I have informed the employee that his/her behavior is unacceptable and will not be tolerated in our company. If this behavior continues, I will be terminating his/her employment relationship.
(Solution) - The employer will require the employee to attend a counseling session with a professional counselor who specializes in workplace harassment issues within _____
days of his/her receipt of this notice. This meeting should be documented in HR records for review by future supervisors.

Approved By: Date

Manager Signature and Title

7. Non-work-related use of the Internet

Many companies have a policy prohibiting employees from sending or receiving personal emails, instant messages or accessing social networking sites (such as Facebook and Twitter) while they are at work. Use the following template for non-work-related use of the Internet:

Date

Employee Name

(Problem Relevance) - Non-Work-Related Email and Instant Message use.

(Problem Cause) - The cause of the employee's violation of our policy is found to actively browsing social media sites during work.

(Problem Analysis) - I observed that he/she sent/received personal emails/instant messages on our company computer during work hours.

(Action Taken) - I have advised him/her that it is against our policy to send/receive personal emails/instant messages on our company computer system while you are working.

(Solution) - The employee will be required to attend a (state type of meeting or training session, such as a counseling or training session). If there is another infarction within _____ months, then the employment relationship may be terminated. If he/she has not violated this policy again within _____ months, then this violation will be removed from his/her personnel file.

Approved By: Date

Manager Signature and Title

8. Personal Calls at Work

For many employees, work is their second home, and they spend more time there than they do at home. This is especially true in workplaces where the employees are allowed to work from home most of the time. In many cases, employees treat the workplace as if it were their own second home and make personal phone calls during working hours. Although this is not a serious enough violation to result in termination, it can lead to a significant loss of productivity if employees are not disciplined for violating this policy. In many companies, personal phone calls at work are not prohibited. In these situations, you may want to define what types of personal phone calls are prohibited and provide employees with an incentive to report violations. In some cases, it may be necessary to communicate your policy regarding personal phone calls at work through email or a memo. Use the following template for personal phone calls at work:

Date

Employee Name

(Problem Relevance) - Employee Personal Phone Calls at Work.

(Problem Cause) - The cause of this employee's personal phone calls is found to be misusing their time to attend personal calls.

(Problem Analysis) - The employee was observed talking on his/her cell phone during working hours.

(Action Taken) - I have advised the employee that it is our policy to prohibit personal calls while working at our office or on our premises. However, telephone calls relating to business matters are permitted during working hours.

(Solution) - The employee will be required to attend a (state type of meeting or training session, such as a counseling or training session).

Approved By: Date

Manager Signature and Title

9. Violation of Company Safety/Security Policy

Employees are expected to follow your company's policies on safety and security. These policies may require specific actions or behaviors from employees. For example, employees may be required to wear safety equipment or carry a weapon at certain times. In addition, employees should understand that they are prohibited from violating the personal safety or security of other employees, customers, or vendors while they are working. Use the following template for violation of company policy on safety and security:

Date

Employee Name

(Problem Relevance) - Violation of Company Policy on Safety and Security.

(Problem Cause) - The cause of the employee's violation is described as carrying illegal weapons in the workplace.

(Problem Analysis) -The employee was observed leaving a work area without wearing his/her safety equipment.

(Action Taken) - I have advised the employee that it is our policy to require employees to wear safety equipment while performing their duties. In addition, I have reminded him/her that we take our policy regarding personal safety very seriously. If he/she does not follow this policy in the future, he/she will be subject to discipline, up to and including termination of employment.

(Solution) - The employee will be required to attend a meeting with me within _____ days to discuss this matter. If he/she does not attend this meeting voluntarily, disciplinary action may be taken against him/her, up to and including termination of employment.

Approved By: Date

Manager Signature and Title

10. Unauthorized use of Email

Many companies have a policy that prohibits employees from using the company email system to send or receive personal messages. Employees should understand this policy and agree to abide by it if they want to work for your company. Although some allow some personal use during lunch or other breaks, it is important to make sure employees understand the company's policy and comply with it. You can do this by posting it in all work areas and talking about it during staff meetings or training sessions. If an employee sends an email or instant message that contains offensive or inappropriate language, then you should write him/her up for violating the company's email policy. If the employee continues to send these messages, then you should terminate the employment relationship. Use the following template for unauthorized use of email:

Date

Employee Name

(Problem Relevance) - Unauthorized Use of Email.
(Problem Cause) - The cause of the employee's unauthorized use of email is described to be sending a personal message during work hours) contrary to our policy.
(Problem Analysis) - Employee X has sent numerous personal messages during work hours and used his/her email account after work hours.
(Action Taken) - I have advised the employee that it is our policy to prohibit employees from using our email accounts for non-work-related purposes. I have also advised him/her

that he/she may be disciplined if he/she violates this policy again.

(Solution) - If there is a repeat violation, then I will issue a written warning and require him/her to attend a counseling session.

(Additional Information) - Employee X has been warned of this policy on previous occasions, so this action is a result of his/her continued failure to comply.

Approved By: Date

Manager Signature and Title

11. Illegally Downloading Software

Employees who illegally download software from the Internet are violating copyright laws, which can result in fines and legal penalties. This type of violation is also particularly difficult for employers to detect because it is hard to tell whether an employee's computer has been infected with a virus or spyware that is downloading the software. However, employers who prohibit illegal downloading of software have a much greater chance of successfully prosecuting an employee who violates this policy if he or she is caught.

When you first make this policy clear to employees, be sure to advise them that you will not tolerate violations and will prosecute any employee who violates this policy. Use the following template for illegally downloading software from the Internet:

Date

Employee Name

(Problem Relevance) - Illegal Downloading of Software from the Internet.

(Problem Cause) - The cause of the employee's illegal downloading activity includes downloading songs and movies. (Problem Analysis) - I observed the employee using his/her computer at his/her desk during lunch. He/she was visiting several websites and downloading files using a peer-to-peer file-sharing program.

(Action Taken) - I have advised the employee that it is illegal to download software and copyrighted music from the Internet. I have also advised him/her that our policy prohibits employees from downloading software and music from the Internet.

(Solution) - The employee will be required to attend a (state type of meeting or training session, such as a counseling or training session).

Approved By: Date

Manager Signature and Title

12. Excessive Use of Sick Days

Employees are expected to be present at work during their scheduled work hours. They are expected to not take more than the allotted number of sick days allowed in your company's policy. If an employee is absent from work for too many days, you should write up the excessive sick days policy violation notification.

An employee might take an excessive number of sick days because he/she does not understand the company policy or because he/she knows that he/she can get away with it. Some employees take sick day after sick day when they are ill and then come back to work when they feel better.

Other employees may use the company's sick day policy as a type of vacation time and do not return until they feel better. If an employee takes sick day after sick day, you should first talk with him/her about the impact on his/her performance and then write him/her up if he/she does not stop taking so many sick days. Use the following template for excessive sick days:

Date

Employee Name

(Problem Relevance) - Excessive Sick Days
(Problem Cause) The cause of this employee's excessive sick days is described to be poor health.
(Problem Analysis) - This employee has _____ (number) days of vacation remaining and _____ (number) days of personal leave that can be used for sick days. He/she does not qualify for FMLA leave, so any future absences need to be sick days.
(Action Taken) - I have spoken with the employee about his/her excessive use of sick days and pointed out the impact on his/her performance. In addition, I have updated the employee's time records to reflect all absences from work due to illness or injury since _____. If he/she does it again, then there will be further disciplinary action. (Solution) - If there are no more violations in _____ weeks, then a written warning will not be necessary. However, if he/she continues to violate this policy after that period, then I will issue a written warning discussing the consequences if there is another violation.

Approved By: Date

Manager Signature and Title

13. Insubordination to a co-worker or supervisor

Insubordination is a type of policy violation that can result in termination. It is one of the most serious violations an employee can commit because it is a direct challenge to you as a manager. An employee will commit insubordination if he/she:

- Refuses to take orders from you or a co-worker.
- Ignores or does not follow instructions from you or a co-worker.
- Disagrees with the way you or another co-worker are doing something but refuses to discuss the matter with you or the other co-worker.
- Does not listen when asked to do something by you or another co-worker.
- Is rude, disrespectful, and/or sarcastic toward you or another co-worker even though he/she knows that it will get him/her in trouble.

Use the following template for insubordinate employee:

Date

Employee Name

(Problem Relevance) - Insubordination
(Problem Cause) The cause of the employee's insubordination is described as refusal of orders from managers.
(Problem Analysis) - The employee has ignored or refused to take instructions from a manager or co-worker on multiple occasions.
(Action Taken) - I have provided the employee with several opportunities to improve his/her performance, but it has not helped. Therefore, I will be terminating his/her employment

unless there is significant improvement within _____ days.

(Solution) - I will terminate his/her employment unless he/she changes his/her attitude and behaves in a professional manner. If he/she does not improve his/her behavior and attitude, then I will terminate his/her employment for cause. If he/she is terminated for cause, it will be difficult for him/her to re-apply for another job at this company.

Approved By: Date

Manager Signature and Title

14. Bullying Co-workers or Customers

Bullying co-workers or customers is one of the most serious policy violations that you will encounter. It is a difficult situation to deal with because co-workers and supervisors in the department may have a close relationship, which can make it difficult to write-up an employee for this behavior. It is also very important that you do not let this behavior go unchecked because if you do, other employees may think that they can bully their co-workers and customers as well. Use the following template for bullying co-workers or customers:

Date

Employee Name

(Problem Relevance) - Bullying Co-Workers or Customers
(Problem Cause) - The cause of the employee's behavior is found to be abusive behavior. (Problem Analysis) - The employee has been observed harassing a co-worker and making rude comments to customers.

(Action Taken) - I have advised the employee that this type of behavior is not acceptable in our workplace and that he/she must stop immediately. If he/she does not stop this behavior, I will consider more serious disciplinary action up to and including termination of employment.

Approved By: Date

Manager Signature and Title

15. Mishandling of Company Material or Property

Employees are expected to use company property in a responsible manner. This expectation includes not stealing, misusing, or destroying property. For example, employees should not take company materials home without the approval of their supervisor and should not take company materials home and sell them for personal profit. In addition, employees should understand that they may be subject to criminal prosecution if they steal goods or other materials from customers or vendors. In addition, you should make sure that your employees know about your policies regarding theft and can explain what is expected of them regarding theft. For example, employees may be required to sign a document stating that they understand the company's policies regarding theft or may need to attend meetings where they are taught about the policies regarding theft. Use the following template for theft of company material or property:

Date

Employee Name

(Problem Relevance) - Mishandling of Company Material or Property

(Problem Cause) - The cause of the employee's violation is found to be negligence.

(Problem Analysis) - An inventory showed that several materials were missing from our storeroom. An investigation revealed that the employee had taken these materials for personal use while he/she worked at our store.

(Action Taken) - I have advised the employee that it is our policy to require employees to return all materials when they leave work and not to take them with them when they leave work for any reason. In addition, I have reminded him/her that we take our policies regarding theft very seriously. If he/she does not follow this policy in the future, he/she will be subject to discipline, up to and including termination of employment.

(Solution) - The employee will be required to attend a meeting with me within _____ days to discuss this matter. If he/she does not attend this meeting voluntarily, disciplinary action may be taken against him/her, up to and including termination of employment.

Approved By: Date

Manager Signature and Title

16. Discrimination Against a Co-worker

Employees are expected to treat other employees with respect regardless of their differences, such as age, gender, ethnicity, or physical condition. This means that employees should not harass other employees based on these differences. For example, it is unacceptable for an employee to make inappropriate or derogatory comments about a co-worker's gender or ethnicity. In addition, employees should not treat other employees differently based on the employee's age. For example, it is unacceptable for an older employee to treat a younger employee with disrespect and vice versa. Use the following template for discrimination against a co-worker:

Date

Employee Name

(Problem Relevance) - Discrimination Against a Co-worker
(Problem Cause) - The cause of the employee's violation is violating policies respecting co-workers.
(Problem Analysis) - The employee made inappropriate comments about a co-worker's gender and age.
(Action Taken) - I have advised the employee that he/she should not make derogatory comments about any other employee. If he/she does not follow this policy in the future, he/she will be subject to discipline up to and including termination.
(Solution) - The employee has agreed to attend a meeting with me within _____ days to discuss this matter. If he/she does not attend this meeting voluntarily, disciplinary action may be taken against him/her, up to and including termination of employment.

Approved By: Date

Manager Signature and Title

17. Harassment of a Co-worker

Employees are expected to treat one another with respect and professionalism. It is a violation of company policy to harass or abuse other employees. Serious issues such as these must be dealt with swiftly by the concerned authorities. Use the following template for violations of company policies on harassment:

Date

Employee Name

(Problem Relevance) - Harassment of Other Employees
(Problem Cause) - The cause of the employee's violation is found to be personal disregard for others.
(Problem Analysis) - The employee was observed making rude comments to a coworker in front of other coworkers at lunchtime.
(Action Taken) - I have advised the employee that this behavior violates our policy against harassment. In addition, I have reminded him/her that we take our policy regarding professional behavior very seriously. If he/she does not follow this policy in the future, he/she will be subject to discipline, up to and including termination of employment.
(Solution) - The employee will be required to attend a meeting with me within _____ days to discuss this matter. If he/she does not attend this meeting voluntarily, disciplinary action may be taken against him/her, up to and including termination of employment.

Approved By: Date

Manager Signature and Title

18. Commercial Conflict of Interest (conflict with own interests or that of company)

Conflicts of interest are unethical situations in which employees use their position to benefit themselves financially or otherwise rather than the company.

Employees who exploit company resources risk their jobs and face fines and/or imprisonment in some cases. In addition, employees should not accept any form of compensation from vendors because they are involved with purchasing from those vendors or supervising others who are involved with purchasing from those vendors. Use the following template for conflict of interest:

Date

Employee Name

(Problem Relevance) - Conflict of Interest.

(Problem Cause) - The cause of this problem is described is a troublesome individual violating policy.

(Problem Analysis) - The employee was observed discussing a product that is made by one of our competitors during a work meeting that he/she was leading. In addition, he/she recommended that we consider buying this product instead of using our current products for our customer.

(Action Taken) - I have advised the employee that actions such as these are unacceptable because they represent a conflict of interest for him/her. In addition, I have reminded him/her that we require all employees to avoid any actions that may even appear to be a conflict of interest with our fiduciary responsibility to our company. If he/she does not follow this policy in the future, he/she will be subject to discipline, up to and including termination of employment.

(Solution) - The employee will be required to attend a meeting with me within _____ days to discuss this matter. If he/she does not attend this meeting voluntarily, disciplinary action may be taken against him/her, up to and including termination of employment.

Approved By: Date
Manager Signature and Title

19. Moonlighting

Employees are not permitted to have another simultaneous job while working for a particular firm during off-hours. This practice is known as moonlighting. Employees who perform work for your company while they are being paid by another company may be more interested in the other company's work than in your company's work. If your employees fail to perform their work for you, it is difficult to take disciplinary action against them. Use the following template for violations of company policy on moonlighting:

Date

Employee Name

(Problem Relevance) - Violation of Company Policy on Moonlighting

(Problem Cause) - The cause of the employee's violation is deemed to be financial reasons.

(Problem Analysis) - The employee was observed working for another company while he/she was on our payroll.

(Action Taken) - I have advised the employee that moonlighting is not permitted by our company. In addition, I have reminded him/her that we will not be responsible for any damages caused by him/her to the other employer's property or work product as a result of his/her moonlighting activities. If he/she fails to follow this policy in the future, he/she will be subject to discipline up to and including termination of employment.

(Solution) - The employee will be required to attend a meeting with me within _____ days to discuss this matter. If he/she does not attend this meeting voluntarily, disciplinary action may be taken against him/her up to and including termination of employment.

Approved By: Date

Manager Signature and Title

20. Substance Abuse

Use the following template for violation of company policy on substance abuse:

Date

Employee Name

(Problem Relevance) - Violation of Company Policy on Substance Abuse
(Problem Cause) - The cause of the employee's violation is found to be drug addiction. (Problem Analysis) - I observed the employee arriving for work at [time] appearing to be under the influence of alcohol or illegal drugs. In addition, I have received reports that the employee has appeared to be under the influence of alcohol or illegal drugs on the following dates: [list dates].
(Action Taken) - I have advised the employee that it is our policy to prohibit employees from using illegal drugs or controlled substances while they are working. In addition, I have reminded him/her that we take our policy regarding substance abuse very seriously. If he/she does not follow this policy in the future, he/she will be subject to discipline, up to and including termination of employment.
(Solution) - The employee will be required to attend a meeting with me within _____ days to discuss this matter. If he/she does not attend this meeting voluntarily, disciplinary action may be taken against him/her, up to and including termination of employment.

Approved By: Date

Manager Signature and Title

21. Employee Work Time Usage Violating Company Policy

Employee time usage not per company policy occurs when an employee does not use his or her time in a way that is consistent with his or her job description. For example, an employee who is supposed to be working on a certain project may be spending too much time in non-work-related activities. Use the following template for violation of company policy on work time usage:

Date

Employee Name

(Problem Relevance) - Violation of Company Policy on Work Time Usage
(Problem Cause) The cause of the violation is found to be improper time management. (Problem Analysis) - On [date], I observed the employee arriving for work at [time] and then leaving for lunch at [time] without asking permission. In addition, I have received reports that the employee has engaged in similar violations on the following dates: [list dates].
(Action Taken) - I have advised the employee that it is our policy not to leave his/her workstation without first checking with their manager. In addition, I have reminded him/her that we take our policy regarding use of company time very seriously. If he/she does not follow this policy in the future, he/she will be subject to discipline, up to and including termination of employment.
(Solution) - The employee will be required to attend a meeting with me within _____ days to discuss this matter. If

he/she does not attend this meeting voluntarily, disciplinary action may be taken against him/her, up to and including termination of employment.

Approved By: Date

Manager Signature and Title

22. Employee Using Racial, Ethnic, or Religious Slurs

Employees who are malicious in using racial, ethnic, or religious slurs may cause serious problems for their employers and fellow employees. These types of slurs create a hostile work environment that can lead to lawsuits that can cost employers a great deal of money. In addition, such slurs violate company policy and can result in discipline up to and including termination of employment. Use the following template for violation of company policy on racial, ethnic, or religious slurs:

Date

Employee Name

(Problem Relevance) - Violation of Company Policy on Racial/Ethnic/Religious Slurs
(Problem Cause) - The cause of the employee's violation is found to be racially motivated.
(Problem Analysis) - On [date], I observed the employee making inappropriate comments about African Americans during a conversation with other employees. In addition, I have received reports that the employee has made similar comments about African Americans on the following dates: [list dates].

(Action Taken) - I have advised the employee that it is our policy to prohibit such comments from being made. If he/she does not follow this policy in the future, she/he will be subject to discipline, up to and including termination of employment. (Solution) - The employee will be required to attend a meeting with me within _____ days to discuss this matter. If he/she does not attend this meeting voluntarily, disciplinary action may be taken against him/her, up to and including termination of employment.

Approved By: Date

Manager Signature and Title

23. Theft of Property Belonging to a Co-worker or Supervisor

Use the following template for violation of company policy on theft:

Date

Employee Name

(Problem Relevance) - Violation of Company Policy on Theft
(Problem Cause) - The cause of the employee's violation is due to past criminal records.
(Problem Analysis) - On [date], I observed the employee taking property belonging to a coworker. The employee was observed placing this property in his/her desk drawer. I have also received reports that the employee has been stealing property belonging to other co-workers. In addition, I have received reports that the employee has been stealing office supplies from the supply room.

(Action Taken) - I have advised the employee that it is our policy to prohibit employees from stealing any items belonging to other co-workers or supervisors. In addition, I have reminded him/her that we take our policy regarding theft very seriously. If he/she does not follow this policy in the future, he/she will be subject to discipline, up to and including termination of employment.

(Solution) - The employee will be required to attend a meeting with me within _____ days to discuss this matter. If he/she does not attend this meeting voluntarily, disciplinary action may be taken against him/her, up to and including termination of employment.

Approved By: Date

Manager Signature and Title

24. Dishonesty

Dishonesty is failing to uphold the standards of integrity and honesty that an organization expects from its employees. Employers place a great deal of trust in their employees, and they expect them not to use that trust for personal gain. Employees who are dishonest not only cheat their employers, but they also violate the public's trust. Dishonesty can take many forms, including falsification of documents, altering records, stealing from the employer or other employees, fraud, and fraudulently obtaining money or property from others. Use the following template for violation of company policy on dishonesty:

Date

Employee Name

(Problem Relevance) - Violation of Company Policy on Dishonesty

(Problem Cause) The cause of the employee's violation is found to be ill intent.

(Problem Analysis) - On [date], I observed the employee arriving for work at [time] with a large amount of cash in his possession. This amount was over and above what he requested when he began working for us. In addition, he has not made any deposits into our bank account, and I have no record of him receiving any payment from other employers. I have also received information that he is not registered for tax purposes with the government.

(Action Taken) - I have advised the employee that it is our policy to prohibit employees from stealing or otherwise obtaining money or property from others. In addition, we do not allow our employees to engage in any form of fraud against our company or other parties. If he/she does not follow this policy in the future, he/she will be subject to discipline up to and including termination of employment.

(Solution) - The employee will be required to attend a meeting with me within _____ days to discuss this matter. If he/she does not attend this meeting voluntarily, disciplinary action may be taken against him/her up to and including termination of employment.

Approved by: Date

Manager Signature and Title

25. Violation of Confidentiality Agreements

Confidentiality agreements are common in businesses that deal with sensitive data such as trade secrets, customer lists, and product designs. Confidentiality agreements may also be included in the employee handbook. An employee who breaks his/her confidentiality agreement may be subject to disciplinary action, up to and including termination of employment. The employee should be informed that the company's trade secrets are expected to remain confidential. Violating the company's policy on trade secrets can result in a loss of profits for the company because other companies could benefit from any information that is disclosed. Use the following template for violation of company policy on confidentiality:

Date

Employee Name

(Problem Relevance) - Violation of Company Policy on Confidentiality
(Problem Cause) - The cause of the employee's violation is due to supporting competitors.
(Problem Analysis) - On [date], I observed the employee discussing confidential information with [name] when he/she should have known that the information was confidential. In addition, I have received reports that the employee has discussed confidential information with [name] on the following dates: [list dates].
(Action Taken) - I have advised the employee that it is our policy to prohibit anyone from disclosing any confidential information to anyone outside this company without prior written approval. In addition, I have reminded him/her that we take our confidentiality policies very seriously. If he/she does not follow this policy in the future, he/she will be subject to discipline up to and including termination of employment.
(Solution) - The employee will be required to attend a meeting with me within _____ days to discuss this matter. If he/she does not attend this meeting voluntarily, disciplinary

action may be taken against him/her, up to and including termination of employment.

Approved By: Date

Manager Signature and Title

26. Exploiting Trade Secrets

Use the following template for violation of company policy on trade secrets:

Date

Employee Name

(Problem Relevance) - Exploiting Company Policy on Trade Secrets

(Problem Cause) - The violation of policies is found to be personal gains.

(Problem Analysis) - I informed the employee that we take our policies regarding trade secrets very seriously and asked him/her to explain what he/she was doing. The employee stated that he/she had been asked by his/her supervisor to [state what the employee was doing]. The explanation is described below:

(Action Taken) - I advised him/her that it is our policy to prohibit employees from disclosing information about our products and processes without proper authorization from their supervisors or management. In addition, I reminded him/her that we take our policy regarding trade secrets very seriously. If he/she does not follow this policy in the future, he/she will be subject to discipline, up to and including termination of employment. (Solution) The employee will be required to attend a meeting with me within _____ days to discuss this matter. If he/she does not attend this meeting voluntarily, disciplinary action may be taken against him/her, up to and including termination of employment.

Approved By: Date

Manager Signature and Title

27. Excessive Absenteeism Without Valid Reason

Some employees call in sick to work when they are not actually ill or hurt. They may use the time off for personal reasons, such as visiting a dying relative or going on vacation. They may also use the time off to have someone else do their job, such as taking their place during the hours that they are at work.

Excessive absenteeism without valid reason is usually considered a form of financial fraud on the employer. This type of absenteeism involves an employee who is absent from work without a valid excuse more than twice during any consecutive three-month period. To record this type of absence accurately, it is important to specify that it is excessive and without valid reason. Use the following template for violation of company policy on excessive absenteeism:

Date

Employee Name

(Problem Relevance) - Excessive Absenteeism Without Valid Reason
(Problem Cause) The cause of the employee's violation is due to personal reasons.
(Problem Analysis) - On [date], the employee was absent from work for _____ hours. According to her manager, this is in

violation of company policy on excessive absenteeism. It should be noted that this is the second instance of excessive absenteeism during a three-month period. (Action Taken) - I advised the employee that we have a strict policy against excessive absenteeism without valid reason. In addition, I told her that we take our policies regarding hiding or destroying evidence very seriously. If she violates this policy in the future, she will be subject to discipline, up to and including termination of employment.

(Solution) - The employee will be required to attend a meeting with me within _____ days to discuss this matter. If she does not attend this meeting voluntarily, disciplinary action may be taken against her, up to and including termination of employment.

Approved By: Date

Manager Signature and Title

28. Infraction of Safety Policy

Employees sometimes violate workplace safety policies. The most common infractions involve failure to wear safety equipment, failure to report unsafe conditions, and failure to follow safety procedures. Use the following template for violation of company policy on infraction of safety policy:

Date

Employee Name

(Problem Relevance) - Violation of Company Policy on Infraction of Safety Policy

(Problem Cause) The cause of the employee's violation is due to negligence.

(Problem Analysis) - On [date], I observed the employee working in an area that was not properly ventilated for [type of work]. When I asked him/her about this, he/she said that he/she did not know there was a problem. (Action Taken) - I advised the employee that we have a strict safety policy that requires him/her to report all unsafe conditions to his/her supervisor so that they can be immediately rectified. In addition, I told him/her not to work in this area until it can be properly ventilated.

(Solution) - The employee will be required to attend a meeting with me within _____ days to discuss this matter. If he/she does not attend this meeting voluntarily, disciplinary action may be taken against him/her, up to and including termination of employment.

Approved By: Date

Manager Signature and Title

29. Deceitful Leverage of Company Information for Personal Gain

Employees may sometimes use their knowledge of company information to their advantage. They may take advantage of this information to benefit themselves in such a way that they gain at the expense of the company. In some cases, employees may tell a customer that their products are "on sale" or mark them down even though such action is contrary to company policy. In other cases, an employee may sell his/her employer's product(s) to another company for a higher price than his/her employer charges for products of similar quality and value. Use the following template for violation of company policy on deceitful leverage of company information:

Date

Employee Name

(Problem Relevance) - Violation of Company Policy on Deceitful Leverage of Company Information for Personal Gain

(Problem Cause) The cause of the employee's violation is due to the employee's deceitfulness.

(Problem Analysis) - On [date], I observed the employee selling our product to another company for a price that exceeds our company's standard price. The product was sold at [time] on [date]. (Action Taken) - I advised the employee that we have a strict policy against employees selling our products to other companies for a price higher than our standard price. In addition, I told him/her that we take this policy very seriously because it directly affects our profits. If he/she violates this policy in the future, he/she will be subject to discipline, up to and including termination of employment. (Solution) - The employee will be required to attend a meeting with me within _____ days to discuss this matter. If he/she does not attend this meeting voluntarily, disciplinary action may be taken against him/her, up to and including termination of employment.

Approved By: Date

Manager Signature and Title

30. Breach of a Standard Operating Procedure

The breach of a standard operating procedure is a form of financial fraud on the employer. This violation occurs when an employee does not follow a company policy or procedure. This is often referred to as "working outside the box." For example, an employee may take a day off work without notifying his/her supervisor. As another example, an employee may falsify his/her time-card by claiming that he/she worked more hours than he/she actually did. Such actions are violations because they are typically considered to be violations of standard operating procedure or policy. Use the following template for violation of company policy on breach of a standard operating procedure:

Date

Employee Name

(Problem Relevance) - Breach of a Standard Operating Procedure
(Problem Cause) The cause of the employee's violation is due to his/her deceitfulness.
(Problem Analysis) - On [date], I observed the employee taking an extended lunch break without notifying his/her supervisor. He took a total of one hour and fifteen minutes for lunch, which was longer than the standard amount of time (one hour). This occurred at [time] on [date] while he was using our company computer. (Action Taken) - I advised the employee that we have a strict policy against employees taking extended lunch breaks without notifying their supervisor or without first getting permission to do so. In addition, I told him/her that we take this policy very seriously because it directly affects our profits. If he/she violates this policy in the future, he/she will be subject to discipline, up to and including termination of employment.
(Solution) - The employee will be required to attend a meeting with me within _____ days to discuss this matter. If he/she does not attend this meeting voluntarily, disciplinary

action may be taken against him/her, up to and including termination of employment.

Approved By: Date

Manager Signature and Title

31. Violation of Privacy Policies and Other Company Policies About Customer Information

The federal government has established a set of laws and regulations that regulate the collection, use, and dissemination of personal information. To comply with these federal laws and regulations, most employers have adopted policies that prohibit employees from disclosing or using customer information without proper authorization. Furthermore, most employers also have set rules that require employees to keep trade secrets confidential.

Employees often violate these because they are unaware of the policies or because they are tempted by the money offered by outsiders to provide customer information. For example, in one case, a company's employee disclosed trade secrets to an outside company when he thought he was being recruited for a new job. The outside company was actually an undercover government agent who was working to uncover insider trading in the stock market. Use the following template for violation of company policies about customer information:

Date

Employee Name

(Problem Relevance) Violation of customer information policies.

(Problem Cause) The cause of the employee's violation is due to negligence.

(Problem Analysis) - On [date], we discovered that the employee had disclosed customer information about one or more of our clients.

(Action Taken) - We have advised the employee that we take our policy regarding customer privacy very seriously and that we will not tolerate further violations of this policy. If he/she does not follow this policy in the future, he/she will be subject to discipline up to and including termination of employment.

(Solution) - The employee will be required to attend a meeting with me within _____ days to discuss this matter. If he/she does not attend this meeting voluntarily, disciplinary action may be taken against him/her, up to and including termination of employment.

Approved By: Date

Manager Signature and Title

32. Violation of Policies or Procedures that Affect the Company's Financial Statements

Employees who violate policies or procedures that affect the company's financial statements can cause financial losses for the company or may lead to incorrect financial information being reported to shareholders, lenders, and regulators. Use the following template for violation of company policy on financial statements:

Date

Employee Name

(Problem Relevance) - Violation of Company Policy on Financial Statements

(Problem Cause) The cause of the employee's violation is due to poor financial skills. (Problem Analysis) - On [date], I observed the employee entering incorrect information into a spreadsheet. In addition, I have received reports that the employee has entered incorrect information into documents used to prepare our financial statements. This information is summarized as follows: [list acts].

(Action Taken) - I have advised the employee that it is our policy to prohibit employees from entering incorrect information into documents used to prepare our financial statements. In addition, I have reminded him/her that we take our policy regarding the preparation of financial statements very seriously. If he/she does not follow this policy in the future, he/she will be subject to discipline, up to and including termination of employment.

(Solution) - The employee will be required to attend a meeting with me within _____ days to discuss this matter. If he/she does not attend this meeting voluntarily, disciplinary action may be taken against him/her, up to and including termination of employment.

Approved By: Date

Manager Signature and Title

33. Falsifying Records or Data to Defraud the Company or its Customers

Employees often use fraudulent means to obtain benefits from the company or its customers. For example, some employees falsify records or data to cover up a mistake or omission, to get out of work, or to take advantage of special opportunities. Sometimes employees misappropriated company funds for personal gain. Other times they falsify records and data to the vendor's advantage. Many times, these kinds of violations are not discovered until an audit or a review of data. Falsifying records is a serious problem for employers because it can lead to financial losses and customer dissatisfaction. It also is a criminal offense under federal and state statutes. Use the following template for violation of company policy on falsification of records:

Date

Employee Name

(Problem Relevance) - Violation of Company Policy on Falsification of Records

(Problem Cause) The cause of the employee's violation is found to be aiding rival companies.

(Problem Analysis) - On [date], I observed the employee entering inaccurate information into our computer system to cover up a mistake. In addition, I have received reports that the employee has entered inaccurate information into our computer system on the following dates: [list dates].

(Action Taken) - I have advised the employee that it is our policy to prohibit employees from falsifying records or data. In addition, I have reminded him/her that we take our policy regarding falsification of records very seriously. If he/she does not follow this policy in the future, he/she will be subject to discipline, up to and including termination of employment.

(Solution) - The employee will be required to attend a meeting with me within _____ days to discuss this matter. If he/she does not attend this meeting voluntarily, disciplinary action may be taken against him/her, up to and including termination of employment.

Approved By: Date
Manager Signature and Title

34. Unsanctioned Release of Proprietary Information

Unauthorized release of proprietary or confidential information can violate the rights of an employer and can be a crime under some circumstances. Employees who release proprietary or confidential information without authorization may damage the company's reputation and their own. Use the following template for violation of company policy on unauthorized release of proprietary or confidential information:

Date

Employee Name

(Problem Relevance) - Unsanctioned Release of Proprietary Information
(Problem Cause) - The cause of the employee's violation is found to be negligence. (Problem Analysis) - On [date], I observed that the employee made copies of our customer list and distributed them to other members of his/her department. I discovered this situation when one of my customers called me and said that he/she received a copy from another member in his/her department. In addition, I have received reports that the employee has released similar lists on [list dates].
(Action Taken) - I have advised the employee that it is our policy to prohibit employees from releasing proprietary or confidential information without authorization. In addition, I have reminded him/her that we take our policy regarding unauthorized release of information very seriously. If he/she does not follow this policy in the future, he will be subject to discipline up to and including termination of employment.
(Solution) - The employee will be required to attend a meeting with me within _____ days to discuss this matter. If he/she does not attend this meeting voluntarily, disciplinary

action may be taken against him/her, up to and including termination of employment.

Approved By: Date

Manager Signature and Title

35. Unauthorized access to network

Some employees may, through their own carelessness or by accident, access the company's computer network without authorization. In some cases, they may gain access to company files or other information. Some employees may use this information to benefit themselves or to harm others. Use the following template for violation of company policy on unauthorized access:

Date

Employee Name

(Problem Relevance) - Violation of Company Policy on Network Access.
(Problem Cause) The cause of the employee's violation is due to the employee's carelessness and/or negligence.
(Problem Analysis) - On [date], I observed the employee accessing the company's computer network without authorization and causing damage to our shared network. The employee accessed the company's computer network on [time] while using the company's computer located in [location]. The employee accessed files that were not authorized for his/her use. In addition, he/she accessed files that he/she was not authorized to access.
(Action Taken) - I advised the employee that we have a strict policy against employees accessing our computer network

without authorization and causing damage to our shared network. In addition, I told him/her that we take this policy very seriously because it directly affects our profits. If he/she violates this policy in the future, he/she will be subject to discipline, up to and including termination of employment.

(Solution) - The employee will be required to attend a meeting with me within _____ days to discuss this matter. If he/she does not attend this meeting voluntarily, disciplinary action may be taken against him/her, up to and including termination of employment.

Approved By: Date

Manager Signature and Title

36. Unauthorized Use of Company Vehicle

Employees who use their company vehicle for personal trips are violating company policy and may be risking the security of their job. If an employee uses a company vehicle for personal use, he/she may be put in a compromising position with respect to his/her employer. For example, if the employee is involved in an accident while using the company vehicle for personal reasons, it could appear that the employee was driving recklessly because he/she was not concerned with his/her job. Or, if a co-worker borrowed the car and was involved in an accident, it could appear that the employee was negligent or had allowed someone else to drive his/her car without permission. While these scenarios are unlikely, they illustrate why employers take unauthorized use of company vehicles very seriously. The following template can be used to document unauthorized use of a company vehicle:

Date
Employee Name

(Problem Relevance) - Violation of Company Policy on Use of Company Vehicles.w

(Problem Cause) The cause of the employee's violation is due to financial motives.

(Problem Analysis) - On [date], I observed the employee driving his/her company vehicle to a personal errand. In addition, I have received reports that the employee used his/her company vehicle for personal reasons on the following dates: [list dates].

(Action Taken) - I have advised the employee that it is our policy to prohibit employees from using company vehicles for personal errands. In addition, I have reminded him/her that we take our policy regarding unauthorized use of company vehicles very seriously. If he/she does not follow this policy in the future, he/she will be subject to discipline, up to and including termination of employment.

(Solution) - The employee will be required to attend a meeting with me within _____ days to discuss this matter. If he/she does not attend this meeting voluntarily, disciplinary action may be taken against him/her, up to and including termination of employment.

Approved By: Date

Manager Signature and Title

Chapter 4: Performance Problems

In this chapter, you will find sample write-ups for performance problems. The write-ups have been written with the intent to be as clear and concise as possible. You will notice that there are only two pages of write-ups instead of the expected four or five pages found in many books on performance management. Our feeling is that performance problems are better handled by short, concise, well-written write-ups. This allows the manager and employee to concentrate on the problem rather than on a lengthy document. The write-ups provided here are not "cookie cutter" documents. As with everything else in this book, they are guidelines from which to develop your own style of writing.

The Background section is designed to provide enough information so that the reader can understand the problem. It should include dates, job titles, salary ranges and any other information that will help clarify the problem. The Problems section is where you will describe what has happened and why you are creating a write-up. The Action Steps section is where you will list what the employee must do to correct the problem and what you expect from them in terms of time frame for correction. You may want to add additional sections if they seem necessary for your situation but always remember, this is your write-up, and if it works better without something listed above, feel free to drop it.

Again, there are no right or wrong answers here as long as the reader is left with a clear understanding of what should happen next in regard to this particular performance problem.

Let's get started!

37. Work Quality and Performance Not Meeting the Standards

Employees who are not performing their jobs in a satisfactory manner may need to be disciplined. Poor performance can result from a wide variety of problems, including (but not limited to): incompetence, lack of skills, lack of effort, poor attitude, poor work habits, or failure to follow instructions. Use the following template for violation of company policy on poor performance:

Date

Employee Name

(Problem Relevance) - Violation of Company Policy on Poor Performance.
(Problem cause)- The employee was observed (state act) in a way that violated our policies regarding poor performance.
(Action Taken) I have advised the employee that he/she is not meeting the standards of performance that we expect for [job title] at this company. In addition, I have reminded him/her of the need to improve his/her performance and set a deadline for improvement. If he/she does not meet acceptable performance standards by [set deadline], I will take further disciplinary action against him/her.

Approved By: Date

Manager Signature and Title

38. Lack of Attention to Detail

Lack of attention to detail is a violation of company policy that can affect the quality of work, the efficiency of operations, and the effectiveness of the employee. For example, if an employee fails to inspect an item before it leaves your facility, you may not discover that it is defective until after it has been delivered to a customer. In some cases, this can lead to costly recalls. Remember, to be effective when documenting violations of company policies on lack of attention to detail, you should align your documentation with your specific organizational goals and objectives. For example, you may want to emphasize different types of violations depending on the type of work the employee is doing. For example, if the employee is responsible for inspecting shipments, the primary areas where you should focus are in packing and shipping. However, if the employee is responsible for handling customer complaints, you may want to focus on such areas as customer service complaints. Use the following template for violation of company policy on lack of attention to detail:

Date

Employee Name

(Problem Relevance) - Violation of Company Policy on Lack of Attention to Detail.

(Problem Cause) The cause of the employee's violation is a lack of knowledge.

(Problem Analysis) - On [date], I observed the employee performing his/her duties in a careless manner and not paying close attention to what he/she was doing. In addition, I have received reports that the employee has been performing his/her duties in a careless manner and not paying close attention to what he/she was doing on the following dates: [list dates].

(Action Taken) - I have advised the employee that it is our policy to require employees to perform his/her duties in a careful and conscientious manner. In addition, I reminded him/her that we take this policy very seriously. If he/she does not follow this policy in the future, he/she will be subject to discipline, up to and including termination of employment.

(Solution) - The employee will be required to attend a meeting with me within _____ days to discuss this matter. If he/she does not attend this meeting voluntarily, disciplinary action may be taken against him/her, up to and including termination of employment.

Approved By: Date

Manager Signature and Title

39. Inability to Follow Directions or to Learn

Inability to follow directions or to learn is an employee's inability or unwillingness to understand and carry out the instructions of the supervisor or other designated authority. Use the following template for violation of company policy on inability to follow directions or learn:

Date

Employee Name

(Problem Relevance) - Violation of Company Policy on Inability to Follow Directions or Learn.
(Problem Cause) The cause of the employee's violation is lack of skills.
(Problem Analysis) - On [date], I observed the employee making a mistake while performing his/her duties. This mistake could have been avoided if he/she had followed my instructions. In addition, I have received reports that he/she has made similar mistakes on the following dates: [list dates].
(Action Taken) - I advised the employee that we expect employees to follow our instructions and obey policies and procedures. If he/she does not do this in the future, he/she

will be subject to discipline up to and including termination of employment.

(Solution) - The employee will be required to attend a meeting with me within _____ days to discuss this matter. If he/she does not attend this meeting voluntarily, disciplinary action may be taken against him/her, up to and including termination of employment.

Approved By: Date

Manager Signature and Title

40. Lack of Motivation

Employees who are not motivated to do their jobs may threaten your ability to run a profitable business. Employees who are apathetic about their work may be less productive and more prone to error. The lack of motivation described may stem from numerous possible causes. For example, it may be that there is disagreement about the employee's job duties, or that he/she is being supervised in an overly critical manner. To address this problem, you should first determine whether the employee is being given clear and adequate instructions and feedback about his/her performance. If not, you should provide clear and specific guidelines for the employee's responsibilities and methods for giving feedback about his/her job performance. Use the following template for violation of company policy on lack of motivation:

Date

Employee Name

(Problem Relevance) - Violation of Company Policy on Lack of Motivation.

(Problem Cause) The employee's lack of motivation is found to be an inept individual. (Problem Analysis) - In [month], the employee failed to complete [number] out of [total number] sales calls that were assigned to him/her. In addition, the manager who oversees this employee informed me that he/she has noticed an overall decrease in the quality and quantity of the employee's work over the past several months.

(Action Taken) - I have advised the employee that it is our policy to require employees to complete all sales calls assigned to him/her each month. In addition, I have informed him/her that his/her performance levels are not acceptable at this time. If his/her performance does not improve, he/she will be subject to discipline up to and including termination of employment.

(Solution) - The employee will be required to meet with me within _____ days for a discussion regarding his/her performance problems. If he/she does not attend this meeting voluntarily, disciplinary action may be taken against him/her up to and including termination of employment.

Approved By: Date

Manager Signature and Title

41. Inadequate Interest to Complete Tasks

Some employees may appear to lack sufficient interest to finish their tasks, even though the completion of those tasks is important enough to warrant their effort. These employees may be seen as lacking motivation or as having low morale. In some cases, such an employee may have an interest in his/her job and in his/her work, but he/she may not be able to motivate himself/herself to perform the tasks that are required to do the job well or to do them correctly. Use the following template for violation of company policy on lack of interest:

Date

Employee Name

(Problem Relevance) - Violation of Company Policy on Lack of Interest in Tasks.

(Problem Cause) The cause of the employee's violation is due to his/her lack of motivation.

(Problem Analysis) - On [date], I observed that the employee seemed uninterested in performing his/her job tasks. For example, it appeared that he/she did not want to do them, and he/she did not make a good-faith effort to complete them correctly. As another example, he/she did not seem motivated enough to finish them on time. (Action Taken) - I advised the employee that we expect all employees to take an active interest in contributing to the smooth operation of our organization. If he/she violates this policy in the future, he/she will be subject to discipline, up to and including termination of employment.

(Solution) - The employee will be required to attend a meeting with me within _____ days to discuss this matter. If he/she does not attend this meeting voluntarily, disciplinary action may be taken against him/her, up to and including termination of employment.

Approved By: Date

Manager Signature and Title

42. Lack of Initiative

Lack of initiative on the part of an employee can be both a cause and effect of low morale. An employee may not be willing to take the initiative to do something because it is not part of his/her job description. In other cases, an employee may avoid doing anything that might involve extra effort because he/she feels that it is not worth his/her time. In either case, the result will be low morale and a decrease in productivity. Use the following template for violation of company policy on lack of initiative:

Date

Employee Name

(Problem Relevance) - Violation of Company Policy on Lack of Initiative.
(Problem Cause) The cause of the employee's violation is due to the employee's lack of motivation.
(Problem Analysis) - On [date], I observed the employee being uncooperative with another staff member by telling him/her to do something that he/she should have done. The incident occurred at [time] on [date]. (Action Taken) - I advised the employee that we expect all employees to act in a cooperative and collegial manner with one another. In addition, I told him/her that we expect all employees to take an active interest in contributing to the smooth operation of our organization. If he/she violates this policy in the future, he/she will be subject to discipline, up to and including termination of employment.
(Solution) - The employee will be required to attend a meeting with me within _____ days to discuss this matter. If he/she does not attend this meeting voluntarily, disciplinary action may be taken against him/her, up to and including termination of employment.

Approved By: Date

Manager Signature and Title

43. Lacking Self-Confidence

Some employees may act in a manner that indicates a lack of self-confidence. They may not appear to be able to make independent decisions, and they may have difficulty prioritizing their work. In some cases, they might perform their job tasks with such little effort that it is clear to others that they lack the motivation necessary for success in their current role. Some employees may act in such a way as to indicate that they do not take their role seriously, even though the job requires them to take their role seriously. Use the following template for violation of company policy on absence of self-confidence:

Date

Employee Name

(Problem Relevance) - Violation of Company Policy on Absence of Self-Confidence.
(Problem Cause) The cause of the employee's violation is due to his/her lack of self-confidence.
(Problem Analysis) - On [date], I observed the employee performing his/her job tasks in a manner that indicates a lack of self-confidence. For example, he/she may be unable to make independent decisions, and he/she may have difficulty prioritizing tasks. As another example, he/she may perform job tasks with little effort, which indicates that he/she does not take his role seriously. (Action Taken) - I advised the employee that we expect all employees to take their roles seriously, and we expect them to do so by performing their

responsibilities with a high level of effort. I also told him/her that his/her performance is unacceptable. If he/she fails to show improvement within _____ days, he/she will be subject to discipline, up to and including termination of employment.

(Solution) - The employee will be required to attend a meeting with me within _____ days to discuss this matter. If he/she does not attend this meeting voluntarily, disciplinary action may be taken against him/her, up to and including termination of employment.

Approved By: Date

Manager Signature and Title

44. Deficiency in Problem-Solving Ability or Critical Thinking Skills

Employees may sometimes have a deficiency in problem-solving ability or critical thinking skills. This deficiency may result in their inability to correctly identify a problem and develop an appropriate solution to it. As a result, their actions may ultimately be contrary to the company's goals and objectives. Use the following template for violation of company policy on deficiency in problem-solving ability:

Date

Employee Name

(Problem Relevance) - Violation of Company Policy on Deficiency in Problem-Solving Ability or Critical Thinking Skills.

(Problem Cause) The cause of the employee's violation is due to a deficiency in his/her problem-solving ability or critical thinking skills.

(Problem Analysis) - On [date], I observed the employee failing to identify and solve a problem correctly. The problem is [statement of the problem]. The employee had been informed about this problem on [date] by [name of person who informed the employee].

(Action Taken) - I advised the employee that we have a strict policy against employees who fail to identify and solve problems correctly. In addition, I told him/her that we take this policy very seriously because it directly affects our performance. If he/she violates this policy in the future, he/she will be subject to discipline.

(Solution) - The employee will be required to attend a meeting with me within _____ days to discuss this matter. If he/she does not attend this meeting voluntarily, disciplinary action may be taken against him/her, up to and including termination of employment.

Approved By: Date

Manager Signature and Title

45. Inability to Work Independently

Inability to work independently is a serious problem for employers because it can lead to low productivity and poor quality of work. In addition, employees who are unable to work independently may be more likely to require supervision, which can be particularly costly for employers. Inability to work independently is more widespread among unskilled and semi-skilled workers than among highly educated or professional workers. Use the following template for violation of company policy on inability to work independently:

Date

Employee Name

(Problem Relevance) - Violation of Company Policy on Inability to Work Independently.

(Problem Cause) - The cause of the employee's violation is described to be a nervous worker.

(Problem Analysis) - On [date], I observed the employee arriving for work at [time] and asked him/her to perform a specific task. He/she was unable to complete this task without my direct assistance. In addition, I have received reports that the employee has been unable to complete tasks without direct assistance from his/her coworkers on the following dates: [list dates].

(Action Taken) - I have advised the employee that it is our policy to prohibit employees from working in ways that require direct assistance from other employees. In addition, I have reminded him/her that we take our policy regarding inability to work independently very seriously. If he/she does not follow this policy in the future, he/she will be subject to discipline, up to and including termination of employment.

(Solution) - The employee will be required to attend a meeting with me within _____ days to discuss this matter. If he/she does not attend this meeting voluntarily, disciplinary action may be taken against him/her, up to and including termination of employment.

Approved By: Date

Manager Signature and Title

46. Inability to Deal with Special Situations or Work under Pressure

If an employee has a history of being unable to deal with special situations or work under pressure, you should be able to document instances when he or she has failed to do so. Often, a peer mentoring program will involve pairing a new employee or an employee with special problems with an experienced employee. The experienced employee will help the new employee or one with special problems by providing advice, guidance, and assistance. This may help the employee with special problems to learn how to deal with the special situations or work under pressure. Use the following template for violation of company policy on inability to deal with special situations or work under pressure:

Date

Employee Name

(Problem Relevance) - Violation of Company Policy on Inability to Deal with Special Situations or Work Under Pressure.

(Problem Cause) - The cause of the employee's violation is due to bad ethics.

(Problem Analysis) - On [date], I observed the employee failing to deal with a special situation in a way that was consistent with our policies regarding ability to handle special situations and ability to work effectively under pressure. In addition, I have received reports that the employee has displayed an inability to deal with special situations on the following dates: [list dates].

(Action Taken) - I have advised the employee that it is our policy for employees to follow our policies regarding ability to handle special situations and ability to work effectively under pressure. If he/she does not follow this policy in the future, he/she will be subject to discipline, up to and including termination of employment.

(Solution) - The employee will be required to be attached to a peer mentoring program within _____ days. If he/she fails to participate in the peer mentoring program within this time frame, disciplinary action may be taken against him/her, up to and including termination of employment.

Approved By: Date

Manager Signature and Title

47. Inability to Handle Complicated Situations or Processes

Inability to handle complicated situations or processes is a violation of company policy. This violation occurs when an employee fails to complete work assignments in a timely manner because he/she does not have the skills, knowledge, or training necessary to perform the tasks. Use the following template for violation of company policy on inability to handle complicated situations or processes:

Date

Employee Name

(Problem Relevance) - Violation of Company Policy on Inability to Handle Complicated Situations or Processes.

(Problem Cause) - The cause of the employee's violation is due to lack of knowledge.

(Problem Analysis) - On [date], I observed that [employee name] was unable to complete his/her assignments in a timely manner because he/she did not have enough knowledge about how our company uses this software program. In addition, I have received reports that the employee has been unable to complete his/her assignments in a timely manner on several occasions because he/she did not know how our company uses this software program.

(Action Taken) - I have advised the employee that it is our policy to require employees to learn about and understand the processes involved in their work assignments before they begin to perform the work. In addition, I have reminded him/her that we take our policies regarding not handling the work in a timely manner very seriously. If he/she does not follow this policy in the future, he/she will be subject to discipline, up to and including termination of employment.

(Solution) - The employee will be required to attend a meeting with the IT department within _____ days to discuss this matter. If he/she does not attend this meeting voluntarily, disciplinary action may be taken against him/her, up to and including termination of employment.

Approved By: Date

Manager Signature and Title

48. Inability to Communicate Clearly and Informatively with Others

Inability to communicate clearly with others in the workplace is a serious problem that can lead to accidents and injuries. Employees who are unable to communicate clearly with other employees, vendors, customers, and members of the general public may cause problems for the company. Use the following template for violation of company policy on inability to communicate clearly and informatively with others:

Date

Employee Name

(Problem Relevance) - Violation of Company Policy on Inability to Communicate Clearly and Informatively with Others.

(Problem Cause) -The cause of the employee's violation is due to lack of communication skills.

(Problem Analysis) - On [date], I observed the employee giving information to the public in a way that was unclear and did not provide adequate information for the customer. In addition, I have received reports that the employee has given unclear and inadequate information to members of the public on other dates: [list dates].

(Action Taken) - I have advised the employee that it is our policy to ensure that all employees give clear and adequate information to customers, vendors, and members of the general public. If he/she does not follow this policy in the future, he/she will be subject to discipline, up to and including termination of employment.

(Solution) - The employee will be required to attend a meeting with me within _____ days to discuss this matter. If he/she does not attend this meeting voluntarily, disciplinary action may be taken against him/her, up to and including termination of employment.

Approved By: Date

Manager Signature and Title

49. Not Meeting Deadlines

Not meeting deadlines is a common form of employee misconduct. This can be a problem for employers in many different areas of the workplace, including production, customer service and administration. In most cases, not meeting deadlines is due to inefficient work habits or poor time management skills. Although you should try to correct this problem by training or counseling the employee in poor work habits, you may have to take disciplinary action if he/she does not improve. Violations of company policies on not meeting deadlines can lead to serious problems in the workplace because it can delay or prevent employees from completing their work on time. Therefore, you should enforce your policies regarding not meeting deadlines consistently and appropriately. Use the following template for violation of company policy on not meeting deadlines:

Date

Employee Name

(Problem Relevance) - Violation of Company Policy on Not Meeting Deadlines.

(Problem Cause) - The cause of the employee's failure to meet these deadlines is lack of motivation.

(Problem Analysis) - On [date], I observed that the employee had failed to complete assignments on time. On [date], I gave the employee an assignment with a deadline of [date]. On [date], I observed that he/she had not completed this assignment. In addition, I have received reports that he/she has missed deadlines in similar situations on the following dates: [list dates].

(Action Taken) - I have advised the employee that he/she must meet our deadlines in the future. If he/she fails to do so, he/she will be subject to discipline, up to and including termination of employment.

(Solution) - The employee will be required to attend a meeting with me within _____ days to discuss this matter. If he/she does not attend this meeting voluntarily, disciplinary action may be taken against him/her, up to and including termination of employment.

Approved By: Date

Manager Signature and Title

50. Failure to Meet Sales Targets

To be successful in business, a company must achieve revenue greater than its cost. Companies accomplish this by selling goods and services to customers. One way to ensure that the company achieves its revenue goals is by setting sales targets for each of its employees. Employees who fail to achieve their sales targets are not meeting their employers' expectations. In some cases, they have not performed well enough to meet the minimum expectations established by their employer. In other cases, they have not performed well enough to meet the expected standard of performance established by their employer. Use the following template for violation of company policy on failure to meet sales targets:

Date

Employee Name

(Problem Relevance) - Violation of Company Policy on Failure to Meet Sales Targets.
(Problem Cause) The cause of the employee's violation is due to the employee's failure to meet minimum expectations.
(Problem Analysis) - On [date], I observed the employee fail to meet his/her sales target. The company had expected him/her to sell [number] units at a rate of [rate] per day. However, he/she sold only [number] units at a rate of [rate].
(Action Taken) - I advised the employee that he/she has not performed well enough to meet our minimum expectations regarding sales targets. In addition, I told him/her that we take

our policies regarding failure to meet sales targets very seriously and take appropriate action against employees who fail to meet minimum performance expectations. If he/she violates this policy in the future, he/she will be subject to discipline, up to and including termination of employment.

(Solution) - The employee will be required to attend a meeting with me within _____ days to discuss this matter. If he/she does not attend this meeting voluntarily, disciplinary action may be taken against him/her, up to and including termination of employment.

Approved By: Date

Manager Signature and Title

51. Poor Time Management Skills

Poor time management skills can be a serious problem for employees, especially if they are the primary point person in a department. If you have an employee who is chronically late for work or missing work without notice, you should issue a written warning. You should also require that the employee meet with you to discuss the problem and develop strategies to improve his or her time management skills.

If the problem continues after you have met with the employee and provided written counseling, you may want to consider issuing a written warning. You may also want to consider demoting your employee if he or she is not able to conform his or her behavior to meet your time management requirements. Written Warning: Employee Time Management Problem

Date

Employee Name

(Problem Relevance) - Employee Time Management Problem.
(Problem Cause) The cause of the employee's problem is a lack of awareness.

(Problem Analysis) - On [date], the employee arrived for work at [time] and was late for a staff meeting held at [time]. In addition, the employee has missed a total of [number] hours of work due to his/her inability to arrive at work on time since [date].

(Action Taken) - I have met with the employee on several occasions to discuss his/her time management problem and have provided him/her with written counseling. However, he/she continues to miss work without notice or arrive late without notice.

(Solution) - The employee will be required to attend a meeting with me within _____ days to discuss this matter. If he/she does not attend this meeting voluntarily, disciplinary action may be taken against him/her, up to and including termination of employment.

Approved By: Date

Manager Signature and Title

52. Tendencies of Insubordination

Some employees may tend to be insubordinate. They may openly challenge and disobey their supervisor's directives and orders. For example, an employee may continually argue with his/her supervisor about what to do or how to do something, thereby delaying the completion of the task at hand. Use the following template for violation of company policy on tendencies of insubordination:

Date

Employee Name

(Problem Relevance) - Tendencies of Insubordination.

(Problem Cause) The cause of the employee's violation is due to an unwillingness to follow orders and/or instructions.

(Problem Analysis) - On [date], I observed the employee arguing with me about how to complete a task.

(Action Taken) - I advised the employee that we have a strict policy against employees arguing with their supervisors about how to complete work assignments. In addition, I told him/her that we take this policy very seriously because it directly affects our productivity. If he/she violates this policy in the future, he/she will be subject to discipline, up to and including termination of employment.

(Solution) - The employee will be required to attend a meeting with me within _____ days to discuss this matter. If he/she does not attend this meeting voluntarily, disciplinary action may be taken against him/her, up to and including termination of employment.

Approved By: Date

Manager Signature and Title

53. Inability to Ask Questions or Seek Help

Employees who lack the interest to ask questions or get help when they need it may fail to meet their job responsibilities. They also may waste time and resources by making mistakes that could have been avoided if they had asked for the help they needed. Use the following template for violation of company policy on inability to ask questions or get help:

Date

Employee Name

(Problem Relevance) - Violation of Company Policy on Inability to Ask Questions or Get Help.

(Problem Cause) - The cause of the issue was due to reluctancy of the worker.

(Problem Analysis) - On [date], I observed the employee attempting to perform his/her duties without having obtained sufficient information or assistance from others. Because he/she did not seek help, he/she was unable to perform his/her duties and wasted time while waiting for information that could have been provided by others. In addition, I have received reports that the employee has failed to ask questions or seek help from others on other dates: [list dates].

(Action Taken) - I have advised the employee that it is our policy to require him/her to provide assistance to coworkers and our customers if needed. In addition, I have reminded him/her that we take our policy regarding lack of initiative very seriously. If he/she does not follow this policy in the future, he/she may be subject to discipline up to and including termination of employment.

(Solution) - The employee will be required to attend a meeting with me within _____ days to discuss this matter. If he/she does not attend this meeting voluntarily, disciplinary action may be taken against him/her up to and including termination of employment.

Approved By: Date

Manager Signature and Title

54. Denial to Accept Criticism

Employees sometimes have difficulty accepting criticism. They may find it difficult to accept even constructive criticism, i.e. criticism that is given with the employee's best interests in mind. Use the following template for violation of company policy on denial to accept criticism:

Date

Employee Name

(Problem Relevance) - Violation of Company Policy on Denial to Accept Criticism.

(Problem Cause) The cause of the employee's violation is due to his/her inability to accept constructive criticism.

(Problem Analysis) - On [date], I observed the employee rejecting my suggestions for improving his/her performance. For example, on [date], I asked him/her to consider using a different approach to resolving customer problems, but he/she refused to accept my suggestion.

(Action Taken) - I advised the employee that we have a strict policy against employees rejecting constructive criticism. In addition, I told him/her that we take this policy very seriously because it directly affects our performance. If he/she violates this policy in the future, he/she will be subject to discipline, up to and including termination of employment.

(Solution) - The employee will be required to attend a meeting with me within _____ days to discuss this matter. If he/she does not attend this meeting voluntarily, disciplinary action may be taken against him/her, up to and including termination of employment.

Approved By: Date

Manager Signature and Title

55. Incompetence in Making Prompt Decisions

Employees are sometimes too incompetent to make prompt decisions. In some cases, they may have difficulty making timely decisions because of their own lack of knowledge or experience. In other cases, they may be reluctant to make timely decisions because of their fear that they will be blamed for any mistakes or errors. During the course of an evaluation, the supervisor should look for signs that an employee is delaying in making a decision. Use the following template for violation of company policy on incompetence in making prompt decisions:

Date

Employee Name

(Problem Relevance) - Violation of Company Policy on Incompetence in Making Prompt Decisions.
(Problem Cause) The cause of the employee's violation is due to incompetence.
(Problem Analysis) - On [date], I observed the employee failing to make prompt decisions about our company's business operations. Specifically, on [date], the employee failed to respond to an e-mail from a customer about a product that we sell. The e-mail was sent at [time] on [date]. The customer contacted me at [time] on [date].
(Action Taken) - I advised the employee that we expect prompt responses from all employees regarding our company's business operations. If he/she fails to respond promptly in the future, he/she may be subject to discipline, up to and including termination of employment.

(Solution) - The employee will be required to attend a meeting with me within _____ days to discuss this matter. If he/she does not attend this meeting voluntarily, disciplinary action may be taken against him/her, up to and including termination of employment.

Approved By: Date

Manager Signature and Title

56. Lack of Cooperative Teamwork

When employees do not work well together or they are not willing to cooperate with each other, this can result in lower quality services for customers. It also can lead to lower productivity and higher costs. Managers will typically need to take disciplinary action against employees for lack of team spirit and cooperation. This is particularly true when employees are not willing to cooperate with each other in performing their duties or when they are not willing to work together as a team. Use the following template for violation of company policy on team spirit and cooperation:

Date

Employee Name

(Problem Relevance) - Violation of Company Policy on Lack of Team Spirit and Cooperation.
(Problem Cause) -The cause of the employee's violation is a lack of interactive skills.
(Problem Analysis) - On [date], I observed that the employee had a serious argument with another employee in our office.
(Action Taken) - I advised the employee that this was unprofessional behavior. He/she should not continue to

behave this way in the future. If he/she does not follow this policy in the future, he/she will be subject to discipline, up to and including termination of employment.

(Solution) - The employee will be required to attend a meeting with me within _____ days to discuss this matter. If he/she does not attend this meeting voluntarily, disciplinary action may be taken against him/her, up to and including termination of employment.

Approved By: Date

Manager Signature and Title

57. Complacent in Meeting Company Goals and Performance Expectations

Some employees are not concerned with the success of their employer's business. They may be content to do their job and receive their paycheck even if their business fails. They may not even care if the company is successful or not. Use the following template for violation of company policy on complacency regarding the company's business goals and performance expectations:

Date

Employee Name

(Problem Relevance) - Violation of Company Policy on Complacent Regarding the Company's Business Goals and Performance Expectations.

(Problem Cause) The cause of the employee's violation is due to the lack of enthusiasm for his/her job.

(Problem Analysis) - On [date], I observed the employee [behavior]. He/she did not seem concerned about the success of our business, and I am concerned that he/she may be complacent regarding this matter.

(Action Taken) - I advised the employee that we have a strict policy against complacency regarding our business goals and performance expectations. In addition, I told him/her that we take this policy very seriously because it affects our company's success. If he/she violates this policy in the future, he/she will be subject to discipline, up to and including termination of employment.

(Solution) - The employee will be required to attend a meeting with me within _____ days to discuss this matter. If he/she does not attend this meeting voluntarily, disciplinary action may be taken against him/her, up to and including termination of employment.

Approved By: Date

Manager Signature and Title

58. Poor Reporting and Following Up on Tasks

When an employee fails to report or follow-up on tasks, he/she may indicate that he/she does not take the job seriously. This is a form of the lack of initiative problem. It may also indicate that the employee is not motivated to succeed in his current role. Use the following template for violation of company policy on poor reporting and following-up on tasks:

Date

Employee Name

(Problem Relevance) - Violation of Company Policy on Poor Reporting and Following Up on Tasks.

(Problem Cause) The cause of the employee's violation is due to his/her lack of motivation.

(Problem Analysis) - On [date], I observed the employee failing to report or follow up on multiple tasks during one day at [time] on [date]. For example, he/she may fail to report on the progress of a project, or he/she may fail to follow up on a task that was assigned to him/her.

(Action Taken) - I advised the employee that we expect all employees to take an active interest in contributing to the smooth operation of our organization. If he/she violates this policy in the future, he/she will be subject to discipline, up to and including termination of employment.

(Solution) - The employee will be required to attend a meeting with me within _____ days to discuss this matter. If he/she does not attend this meeting voluntarily, disciplinary action may be taken against him/her, up to and including termination of employment.

59. Unfavorable Handling of Difficult Customers

Some employees do not handle difficult customers well. They may antagonize customers by arguing with them, by insisting on making a sale when the customer does not want to buy, or by giving the customer an inferior product or service in response to the customer's complaint. In some cases, the employee may even lose a valuable customer because of his/her ineptitude in handling difficult customers. Use the following template for violation of company policy on handling difficult customers:

Date

Employee Name

(Problem Relevance) - Violation of Company Policy on Handling Difficult Customers.

(Problem Cause) The cause of the employee's violation is due to his/her poor relationship-building skills.

(Problem Analysis) - On [date], I observed the employee arguing with a customer who was complaining about the employee's service. The customer left our store in an angry state at [time] on [date].

(Action Taken) - I advised the employee that we have a strict policy against employees arguing with customers. In addition, I told him/her that we take this policy very seriously because it can affect our profits and the quality of our customer service. If he/she violates this policy in the future, he/she will be subject to discipline, up to and including termination of employment.

(Solution) - The employee will be required to attend a meeting with me within _____ days to discuss this matter. If he/she does not attend this meeting voluntarily, disciplinary action may be taken against him/her, up to and including termination of employment.

Approved By: Date

Manager Signature and Title.

60. Poor Customer Service

Poor customer service is the failure to provide customers with the level of service they expect. Poor customer service may result in customers switching to a competitor's product or service. It also can result in loss of revenue because customers choose to shop elsewhere. Use the following template for violation of company policy on poor customer service:

Date

Employee Name

(Problem Relevance) - Violation of Company Policy on Poor Customer Service.

(Problem Cause) - The cause of the employee's violation is due to poor communication skills.

(Problem Analysis) - On [date], I observed the employee providing poor customer service to a customer. In addition, I have received reports that the employee has provided poor customer service to customers on the following dates: [List dates].

(Action Taken) - I have advised the employee that it is our policy to provide customers with excellent customer service whenever they interact with us. In addition, I have reminded him/her that we take our policy regarding customer service very seriously. If he/she does not follow this policy in the future, he/she will be subject to discipline, up to and including termination of employment.

(Solution) - The employee will be required to attend a meeting with me within _____ days to discuss this matter. If he/she does not attend this meeting voluntarily, disciplinary action may be taken against him/her, up to and including termination of employment.

Approved By: Date

Manager Signature and Title

61. Excessive Mistakes in Completed Work

High error in work is the failure to follow established safety rules and procedures or to comply with a standard of quality. Use the following template for violation of company policy on excessive mistakes in work:

Date

Employee Name

(Problem Relevance) - Violation of Company Policy on Excessive Mistakes in Work.

(Problem Cause) – The cause of the employee's violation is due to negligence.

(Problem Analysis) - On [date], I observed that the employee neglected to follow safety procedures when performing his/her job duties. As a result, he/she was responsible for [list] serious injuries or accidents that were narrowly avoided. In addition, I have received reports that the employee has made high numbers of errors on the following dates: [list dates].

(Action Taken) - I have advised the employee that it is our policy to require employees to follow safety procedures when they are performing their job duties. In addition, I have reminded him/her that we take our policy regarding high error in work very seriously. If he/she does not follow this policy in the future, he/she will be subject to discipline, up to and including termination of employment.

(Solution) - The employee will be required to attend a meeting with me within _____ days to discuss this matter. If he/she does not attend this meeting voluntarily, disciplinary action may be taken against him/her, up to and including termination of employment.

Approved By: Date

Manager Signature and Title

62. Inefficient Quality of Work

Use the following template for violation of company policy on slow and inefficient work performance:

Date

Employee Name

(Problem Relevance) – Inefficient Quality of Work.

(Problem Cause) - The cause of the employee's violation is found to be lack of quality management skills.

(Problem Analysis) - The employee has a history of working slowly. In addition, he/she has been criticized by coworkers and customers because of his/her slow work. Hours after he/she is assigned to a project, he/she often has finished only a portion of it. On [date], I observed the employee working very slowly. In addition, I have received reports that he/she worked slowly on the following dates: [list dates].

(Action Taken) - I advised the employee that it is our policy to require employees to complete their assigned tasks in a timely manner. If this policy is not followed, we will take disciplinary action against him/her up to and including termination of employment. We expect all employees to meet this standard for completing their work regardless of their position in the company or the amount of money they make. If this policy is not followed, we will take disciplinary action against him/her up to and including termination of employment.

(Solution) - The employee will be required to meet with me within _____ days to discuss this matter. If he/she does not attend this meeting voluntarily, disciplinary action may be taken against him/her up to and including termination of employment.

Approved By: Date

Manager Signature and Title

63. Refusal to Adhere to Working Schedule

An employee who refuses to adhere to his/her working schedule is violating company policy and will likely be considered an unsatisfactory employee. An employee may refuse to adhere to his/her working schedule for a variety of reasons, including personal reasons or illness. The following template can be used for violation of company policy on refusal to adhere to working schedule:

Date

Employee Name

(Problem Relevance) - Violation of Company Policy on Working Schedules.

(Problem Cause) The cause of the employee's violation is due to an unwillingness on his/her part to adhere to the established work schedule.

(Problem Analysis) - On [date], I observed the employee failing or refusing to work the scheduled hours. (Action Taken) - I explained that we expect all employees to adhere to our established work schedule. I further explained that when an employee refuses to work the schedule, he/she is disrupting the productivity of other employees and is unacceptable. If he/she does not show improvement within _____ days, he/she will be subject to discipline, up to and including termination of employment.

(Solution) - The employee will be required to attend a meeting with me within _____ days to discuss this matter. If he/she does not attend this meeting voluntarily, disciplinary action may be taken against him/her, up to and including termination of employment.

Approved By: Date

Manager Signature and Title

Chapter 5: Behavior and Conduct Problems

In the previous chapter we looked at examples of employee performance problems that are primarily due to deficiencies in the employee's ability. In this chapter we will look at examples of employee performance problems that are primarily due to deficiencies in the employee's behavior and conduct.

There is an important distinction between a deficiency in an employee's ability and a deficiency related to their behavior or conduct. When employees demonstrate inability, it is often easy for the employer to identify what went wrong, and why there was a problem. When employees demonstrate deficiencies related to their behavior or conduct, however, this can be more difficult to identify, as there is no specific incident or event that led to the problem. Instead, there may be a series of events that resulted in behavioral issues on behalf of the employee which need to be addressed before the problem can be resolved.

The following examples will help you to better understand employee performance problems that are primarily due to deficiencies in an employee's behavior or conduct.

64. Poor Workplace Attitude

Poor workplace attitude is the inappropriate expression of negative thoughts and feelings toward co-workers, supervisors, vendors, or customers. These expressions are not only insulting and disruptive to other employees, but they can also result in a loss of customer loyalty. Use the following template for violation of company policy on poor workplace attitude:

Date

Employee Name

(Problem Relevance) - Violation of Company Policy on Poor Workplace Attitude .

(Problem Cause) - The cause of the employee's violation is poor attitude.

(Problem Analysis) - On [date], I observed the employee making a negative comment about [name] to another employee. In addition, I have received reports that the employee has made negative comments about [name] on the following dates: [list dates].

(Action Taken) - I have advised the employee that it is our policy to prohibit employees from displaying a poor work environment attitude toward their co-workers or supervisors. In addition, I have reminded him/her that we take our policy regarding poor workplace attitude very seriously. If he/she does not follow this policy in the future, he/she will be subject to disciplinary action, up to and including termination.

(Solution) - The employee will be required to attend a meeting with me within _____ days to discuss this matter. If he/she does not attend this meeting voluntarily, disciplinary action may be taken against him/her, up to and including termination.

Approved By: Date

Manager Signature and Title

65. Inappropriate Interpersonal Relationships

Employees may sometimes engage in negative interpersonal relationships with their coworkers and supervisors. To some degree, most employees will engage in some negative or unpleasant interpersonal relationships with coworkers and supervisors at one time or another. However, there is a difference between an employee who engages in an occasional negative relationship with another employee and an employee who is involved in a string of ongoing negative interpersonal relationships. An employee might engage in a string of ongoing negative interpersonal relationships to the point where his/her behavior negatively affects the workplace environment and the productivity of the organization. Use the following template for violation of company policy on interpersonal relationships:

Date

Employee Name

(Problem Relevance) - Violation of Company Policy on Interpersonal Relationship Skills.
(Problem Cause) The cause of the employee's violation is due to the employee's violation of company policy.
(Problem Analysis) - On [date], I observed the employee engage in a negative interpersonal relationship with coworker [name]. The last time this occurred was on [date], when the employee engaged in this behavior with coworker [name]. On that date, the employee told coworker [name] to "get out" of his/her way.
(Action Taken) - I advised the employee that we have a strict policy against employees engaging in negative interpersonal relationships. In addition, I told him/her that we take this policy very seriously because it directly affects our morale and productivity. If he/she violates this policy in the future, he/she will be subject to discipline, up to and including termination of employment.
(Solution) - The employee will be required to attend a meeting with me within _____ days to discuss this matter. If

he/she does not attend this meeting voluntarily, disciplinary action may be taken against him/her, up to and including termination of employment.

Approved By: Date

Manager Signature and Title

66. Limited Interpersonal Skills

The inability to communicate effectively with others is a serious managerial problem. An employee who lacks interpersonal skills may cause conflict among the company's employees, customers, and/or suppliers. Such conflict may result in the loss of business or clients, financial loss due to bad business deals, or legal action against the company. Use the following template for violation of company policy on limited interpersonal skills:

Date

Employee Name

(Problem Relevance) - Violation of Company Policy on Limited Interpersonal Skills.
(Problem Cause) The cause of the employee's violation is due to his/her limited interpersonal skills.
(Problem Analysis) - On [date], I observed the employee making a rude comment to a customer regarding the customer's choice of products. The comment was made at [time] on [date].
(Action Taken) - I advised the employee that we have a strict policy against employees being rude to any of our customers, our suppliers, or other employees. In addition, I told him/her that we take this policy very seriously because it directly affects

our business deals. If he/she violates this policy in the future, he/she will be subject to discipline, up to and including termination of employment.

(Solution) - The employee will be required to attend a meeting with me within _____ days to discuss this matter. If he/she does not attend this meeting voluntarily, disciplinary action may be taken against him/her, up to and including termination of employment.

Approved By: Date

Manager Signature and Title

67. Inappropriate Tone in Workplace

When employees use inappropriate language or tone, they may offend customers, co-workers or vendors. The perception of the employee's behavior may be more important than the actual words used. Use the following template for violation of company policy on appropriate language or tone:

Date

Employee Name

(Problem Relevance) - Violation of Company Policy on Appropriate Tone.
(Problem Cause) - The cause of the employee's violation is an angry mentality.
(Problem Analysis) - On [date], I observed the employee arrive for work at [time] and was speaking to me while using profanity. [Employee's name] also is reported to have used profanity on the following dates: [list dates]. In addition, I have

received several complaints from other employees that he/she has used profanity while they were working with him/her.

(Action Taken) - I have advised the employee that it is our policy to require employees to refrain from using inappropriate language while they are working. In addition, I have reminded him/her that we take our policy regarding inappropriate language very seriously. If he/she does not follow this policy in the future, he/she will be subject to discipline, up to and including termination of employment.

(Solution) - The employee will be required to attend a meeting with me within _____ days to discuss this matter. If he/she does not attend this meeting voluntarily, disciplinary action may be taken against him/her, up to and including termination of employment.

Approved By: Date

Manager Signature and Title

68. Physical Aggression

Physical aggression is a form of violent workplace aggression that involves a worker's inappropriate behavior directed at another worker. It can occur when a worker makes a threat to the co-worker's safety, or when a worker makes false accusations against another worker. It also can occur when one worker spreads rumors about another worker. Use the following template for violation of company policy on physical aggression:

Date

Employee Name

(Problem Relevance) - Violation of Company Policy on Physical Aggression.

(Problem Cause) - The cause of the employee's violation is found to be anger issues.

(Problem Analysis) - On [date], I observed the employee attempting to abuse [another employee name]. In addition, several employees have reported that the employee has been abusive to them on the following dates: [list dates].

(Action Taken) - I have advised the employee that it is our policy to prohibit employees from behaving in this manner. In addition, I have reminded him/her that we take our policy regarding verbal aggression very seriously. If he/she does not follow this policy in the future, he/she will be subject to discipline, up to and including termination of employment.

(Solution) The employee will be required to attend a meeting with me within _____ days to discuss this matter. If he/she does not attend this meeting voluntarily, disciplinary action may be taken against him/her, up to and including termination of employment.

Approved By: Date

Manager Signature and Title

69. Verbal Abuse

Verbal abuse is any conduct that is disrespectful or unacceptable to others, including employees, customers, vendors, and supervisors. Verbal abuse can include offensive language, threats, yelling, and racial or sexual slurs. Verbal abuse by an employee can affect the performance of other employees. Therefore, verbal abuse can cause a company to lose customers and may result in a decline in productivity. Use the following template for violation of company policy on verbal abuse:

Date

Employee Name

(Problem Relevance) - Violation of Company Policy on Verbal Abuse.

(Problem Cause) - The cause of the employee's violation is described below:

(Problem Analysis) On [date], I observed the employee repeatedly using inappropriate language while speaking to an employee in another department. In addition, I have received reports that the employee has used inappropriate language with other employees on a number of occasions. For example: [list dates].

(Action Taken) - I have advised the employee that it is our policy to prohibit him/her from using any type of offensive language or gestures while he/she is working. In addition, I have reminded him/her that we take this policy very seriously and if he/she does not follow it in the future, he/she will be subject to disciplinary action up to and including termination of employment.

(Solution) - The employee will be required to attend a meeting with me within _____ days to discuss this matter. If he/she does not attend this meeting voluntarily, disciplinary action may be taken against him/her, up to and including termination of employment.

Approved By: Date

Manager Signature and Title

70. Harmful Work Ethics

Employees sometimes fail to comply with their employer's standards of conduct and guidelines for work ethics. This type of violation can often be considered illegal if the employee is not following the standards and guidelines outlined in the company's employee handbook or other related literature, such as employment contracts. For example, an employee may be required to provide a minimum number of work hours each week. The following day, he/she may arrive at work late and claim that he/she was ill while not providing proper documentation to prove his/her illness. Use the following template for violation of company policy on work ethics:

Date

Employee Name

(Problem Relevance) - Violation of Company Policy on Work Ethics.
(Problem Cause) The cause of the employee's violation is due to the employee's lack of work ethics.
(Problem Analysis) - On [date], I observed the employee arriving for work at [time] while claiming that he/she was "ill." However, he/she was not able to provide any documentation to support his/her claim of illness. In addition, he/she arrived at work late despite having adequate time to prepare for his/her shift.
(Action Taken) - I advised the employee that we have a strict policy against employees arriving late for work or claiming that they were ill while not providing proper documentation to prove their illness. In addition, we have a zero-tolerance policy regarding violations of work ethics. If he/she violates this policy in the future, he/she will be subject to discipline, up to and including termination of employment.

(Solution) - The employee will be required to attend a meeting with me within _____ days to discuss this matter. If he/she does not attend this meeting voluntarily, disciplinary action may be taken against him/her, up to and including termination of employment.

Approved By: Date

Manager Signature and Title

71. Workplace Subjugation

Employees sometimes use a subordinate employee in a way to benefit themselves. In some cases, an employee may assign his/her subordinate to perform a task that he/she is not qualified to do. In other cases, an employee may assign his/her subordinate to perform a task that he/she does not want to do. In both situations, the employee benefits himself by assigning the task to another employee who is required to complete it. Use the following template for violation of company policy on workplace subjugation:

Date

Employee Name

(Problem Relevance) - Violation of Company Policy on Workplace Subjugation.
(Problem Cause) The cause of the violation is due to the employee's desire to avoid doing a task.
(Problem Analysis) - On [date], I observed the employee assigning a task to another employee that he/she is not qualified to perform. The task was assigned at [time] on [date]. In addition, I told him/her that we take this policy very seriously because it directly affects our company's bottom line.

If he/she violates this policy in the future, he/she will be subject to discipline, up to and including termination of employment.

(Action Taken) - The employee will be required to attend a meeting with me within _____ days to discuss this matter. If he/she does not attend this meeting voluntarily, disciplinary action may be taken against him/her, up to and including termination of employment.

(Solution) - The employee will be required to complete a course on workplace subjugation within _____ days of returning from the meeting.

Approved By: Date

Manager Signature and Title

72. Defamation of Co-Workers

Defamation of co-workers is a violation of company policy and occurs when an employee makes untrue statements about a fellow employee. In most cases, defamation of co-workers is a form of harassment. You can avoid having to deal with the problem by clearly communicating your policies on harassment to employees at the time they are hired and on a regular basis thereafter. Use the following template for violation of company policy on defamation of co-workers:

Date

Employee Name

(Problem Relevance) - Violation of Company Policy on Defamation of Co-Workers.
(Problem Cause) The cause for this problem is bad attitude.

(Problem Analysis) - On [date], I observed the employee making remarks that were not true regarding his/her coworker and that are intended to harm her reputation. He/she stated, "Mary's work is never done properly," "Mary doesn't know how to do her job," "Mary has no idea what he/she is doing," and "Mary is an incompetent worker." In addition, I have received reports that the employee has made similar remarks on the following dates: [list dates].

(Action Taken) - I have advised the employee that it is our policy to prohibit employees from making false statements about co-workers. In addition, I have reminded him/her that we take our policy regarding defamation of co-workers very seriously. If he/she does not follow this policy in the future, he/she will be subject to discipline up to and including termination of employment.

(Solution) -The employee will be required to attend a meeting with me within _____ days to discuss this matter. If he/she does not attend this meeting voluntarily, disciplinary action may be taken against him/her, up to and including termination of employment.

Approved By: Date

Manager Signature and Title

73. Inappropriate Job-Related Socializing

Inappropriate job-related socializing is the inappropriate or unprofessional interaction between employees. This type of behavior can cause a severe disruption in workflow, create an atmosphere of suspicion and mistrust, and can lead to conflicts between co-workers. Use the following template for violation of company policy on inappropriate job-related socializing:

Date

Employee Name

(Problem Relevance) - Violation of Company Policy on Inappropriate Job-Related Socializing.

(Problem Cause) - The cause of the employee's violation is nervousness.

(Problem Analysis) - On [date], I observed the employee joining a conversation among other employees who were talking about their personal lives during work hours. In addition, I have received reports that the employee has engaged in inappropriate socializing with other employees on the following dates: [list dates].

(Action Taken) - I have advised the employee that it is our policy to prohibit employees from engaging in inappropriate job-related socializing while they are working. In addition, I have reminded him/her that we take our policy regarding appropriate work conduct very seriously. If he/she does not follow this policy in the future, he/she will be subject to discipline.

(Solution) - The employee will be required to attend a meeting with me within _____ days to discuss this matter. If he/she does not attend this meeting voluntarily, disciplinary action may be taken against him/her.

Approved By: Date

Manager Signature and Title

74. Unprofessional Conduct in the Workplace

Unprofessional conduct is any action or behavior which is unbecoming to a professional person in the community. A person's behavior can be considered unprofessional when it is inconsistent with generally accepted standards of conduct in a business, industry, or occupation. Examples of unprofessional conduct in the workplace include:

- Verbal abuse of coworkers, managers, other employees, or customers
- Eating or drinking in areas where food and beverages are prohibited.
- Having inappropriate personal items on display at work. For example, using a cell phone while working or keeping family photos on the desk.
- Arriving late for work or arriving for work when intoxicated. (This is also considered substance abuse.)
- Failing to follow company dress code policies. This includes not wearing a uniform or other required clothing that is appropriate for the job. It also includes wearing clothing that is inappropriate for the job such as earrings for men and skirts above the knee for women.

Use the following template to document unprofessional conduct by an employee:

Date

Employee Name

(Problem Relevance) - Unprofessional Conduct.
(Problem Cause) - The causes of the employee's unprofessional conduct are an attitude problem.
(Problem Analysis) On [date], I observed the employee engaging in behavior that was unbecoming to a professional person in the community. The following is a list of dates on which I observed this conduct: [list dates]. In addition, it has

been reported to me that the employee has engaged in similar behavior on the following dates: [list dates]. I have discussed this issue with the employee and informed him/her that we do not tolerate this type of behavior at this company. If he/she engages in similar behavior in the future, he/she may be subject to disciplinary action up to and including termination of employment.

(Action Taken) - If this type of conduct occurs again, I will discuss it with the employee and advise him/her that if it happens again, he/she will be subject to disciplinary action up to and including termination of employment.

(Solution) The employee will be required to attend a meeting with me within _____ days to discuss this matter. If he/she does not attend this meeting voluntarily, disciplinary action may be taken against him/her, up to and including termination of employment.

Approved By: Date

Manager Signature and Title

75. Inappropriate Choice of Clothing

Employees may sometimes choose to wear clothing that is contrary to company policy. Such clothes can be considered unprofessional and may be offensive to customers, clients, or other employees. In some cases, the clothing may not meet the expectations of customers or clients. For example, an employee may wear a shirt with a profanity on it to work. In another case, an employee may wear shorts that are too short to work. Use the following template for violation of company policy on inappropriate choice of clothing:

Date

Employee Name

(Problem Relevance) - Violation of Company Policy on Inappropriate Choice of Clothing.

(Problem Cause) The cause of the employee's violation is due to the employee's unprofessionalism.

(Problem Analysis) - On [date], I observed the employee wearing a shirt with a [profanity] on it. The employee wore this shirt to work on [date].

(Action Taken) - I advised the employee that we have a strict policy against employees wearing clothing with a profanity on it to work. In addition, I told him/her that we take our policies regarding inappropriate choice of clothing very seriously, and that he/she will be subject to discipline, up to and including termination of employment, if he/she violates this policy in the future.

(Solution) - The employee will be required to attend a meeting with me within _____ days to discuss this matter. If he/she does not attend this meeting voluntarily, disciplinary action may be taken against him/her, up to and including termination of employment.

Approved By: Date

Manager Signature and Title

76. Possession of Prohibited Personal Belongings

Employees may possess personal belongings in the workplace that are prohibited by company policy. In some cases, an employee may bring a pet to work. In other cases, an employee may bring food or drink from home into the workplace. Use the following template for violation of company policy on possession of prohibited personal belongings:

Date

Employee Name

(Problem Relevance) - Violation of Company Policy on Possession of Prohibited Personal Belongings.

(Problem Cause) The cause of the employee's violation is due to the employee's blatant disregard for company policy and/or a lack of concern for other employees' well-being.

(Problem Analysis) - On [date], I observed the employee bringing his/her pet to work on [date].

(Action Taken) - I advised the employee that we have a strict policy against employees bringing pets to work. In addition, I told him/her that we take this policy very seriously because pets may cause health problems for other employees. If he/she violates this policy in the future, he/she will be subject to discipline, up to and including termination of employment.

(Solution) - The employee will be required to attend a meeting with me within _____ days to discuss this matter. If he/she does not attend this meeting voluntarily, disciplinary action may be taken against him/her, up to and including termination of employment.

Approved By: Date

Manager Signature and Title

77. Religious Symbols at Work

Working in an environment that is not free from religious symbols can be a violation of the employee's rights. Employees have the legal right to work in a workplace that is free from religion. This means that an employer cannot discriminate against its employees because of their religious beliefs. However, the employer can display religious symbols in its workplace if it does so without discriminating against the employees based on their religion. Some employers may be reluctant to remove all religious symbols from their workplaces because they believe that doing so would violate their employees' freedom of religion. However, displaying any symbol that may seem offensive or discriminatory to some individuals is usually considered a violation of state or federal laws regarding discrimination. Use the following template for violation of company policy on religious symbols at work:

Date

Employee Name

(Problem Relevance) - Violation of Company Policy on Displaying Religious Symbols at Work.
(Problem Cause) The cause of the employee's violation is due to discrimination.
(Problem Analysis) - On [date], I observed the employee displaying the following religious symbol in his/her personal work area: _____.
(Action Taken) - I advised the employee that we have a strict policy against employees displaying religious symbols in our workplace because it may be offensive to some of our employees. In addition, I told him/her that we take this policy very seriously because it may violate state or federal laws regarding discrimination. If he/she violates this policy in the future, he/she will be subject to discipline, up to and including termination of employment.
(Solution) - The employee will be required to attend a meeting with me within _____ days to discuss this matter. If he/she does not attend this meeting voluntarily, disciplinary

action may be taken against him/her, up to and including termination of employment.

Approved By: Date

Manager Signature and Title

78. Unprofessional Gestures at Work

Employees often use profanity, or unprofessional gestures at work. If a manager is aware of this type of behavior, he/she should investigate the situation. Oftentimes, an employee will use profanity or inappropriate language because he/she does not know how to communicate in a more professional manner. In these situations, a supervisor may want to give the employee feedback on how they can fix the problem. Use the following template for violation of company policy on unprofessional language:

Date

Employee Name

(Problem Relevance) - Violation of Company Policy on Unprofessional Gestures.
(Problem Cause) - The cause of the employee's violation is to incite distortedness.
(Problem Analysis) On [date], I observed the employee using profane language while he/she was working with [name] and another employee in your department. I also heard reports that he uses inappropriate language while performing his duties on other occasions as well. For example, I have heard that on several occasions at work parties, the employee has made inappropriate comments.

(Action Taken) I have advised the employee that it is our policy to prohibit such language at work. In addition, I have reminded him/her that we take our policy regarding professionalism at work very seriously. If he/she does not follow this policy in the future, he/she will be subject to discipline, up to and including termination of employment. (Solution) The employee will be required to attend a meeting with me within _____ days to discuss this matter. If he/she does not attend this meeting voluntarily, disciplinary action may be taken against him/her, up to and including termination of employment.

Approved By: Date

Manager Signature and Title

79. Disruptive Behavior in the Workplace

Disruptive Behavior in the Workplace is behavior that disrupts the normal operation of the company. Disruptive behavior can include such things as abusive treatment of fellow employees, unauthorized use of company property, failure to follow safety rules or policies, failure to follow instructions, and failure to meet job expectations. Physical aggression in the workplace is an act of violence or physical force that intentionally hurts or threatens to hurt another person. Physical aggression can take many forms, including hitting, kicking, shoving, punching, spitting on, throwing objects at and sexual assault. Use the following template for violation of company policy on disruptive behavior in the workplace:

Date

Employee Name

(Problem Relevance) - Violation of Company Policy on Disruptive Behavior in the Workplace.

(Problem Cause) - The cause of the employee's violation is a disruptive attitude.

(Problem Analysis) - On [date], I observed the employee engaging in disruptive behavior by yelling at other employees. In addition, I have received reports that the employee has engaged in disruptive behavior on the following dates: [list dates].

(Action Taken) - I have advised the employee that it is our policy to prohibit abusive treatment of fellow employees and that such behavior will not be tolerated. In addition, I have reminded him/her that we take this policy very seriously. If he/she engages in this behavior again, he/she will be subject to discipline up to and including termination of employment.

(Solution) - The employee will be required to attend a meeting with me within _____ days to discuss this matter. If he/she does not attend this meeting voluntarily, disciplinary action may be taken against him/her, up to and including termination of employment.

Approved By: Date

Manager Signature and Title

80. Spreading Fake Rumors

Some employees will spread rumors to hurt their employer. In some cases, these employees may spread rumors about the company's sales figures, profits, or financial health. In other cases, they may spread rumors about a particular manager's performance or character. Use the following template for violation of company policy on spreading fake rumors:

Date

Employee Name

(Problem Relevance) - Violation of Company Policy on Spreading Fake Rumors.

(Problem Cause) The cause of the employee's violation is due to his/her dishonesty and deceitfulness.

(Problem Analysis) - On [date], I observed the employee spreading false information about our company's sales figures, profits, or financial health. He/she told [name of person who heard the false information] that [specific details of the false information].

(Action Taken) - I advised the employee that we take spreading rumors about our company very seriously. If he/she violates this policy in the future, he/she will be subject to discipline, up to and including termination of employment.

(Solution) - The employee will be required to attend a meeting with me within _____ days to discuss this matter. If he/she does not attend this meeting voluntarily, disciplinary action may be taken against him/her, up to and including termination of employment.

Approved By: Date

Manager Signature and Title

81. Fraternizing with Superiors

Some employees may attempt to get close to their superiors to get special favors. In some cases, they may seek personal favors that are not related to work, such as a pay raise or promotion. In other cases, they may socialize with their superiors outside of work when they are supposed to be working. Use the following template for violation of company policy on fraternizing with superiors:

Date

Employee Name

(Problem Relevance) - Violation of Company Policy on Fraternizing with Superiors.

(Problem Cause) The cause of the employee's violation is due to his/her dishonesty and deceitfulness.

(Problem Analysis) - On [date], I observed the employee socializing with his/her superiors at [location].

(Action Taken) - I advised the employee that we have a strict policy against employees socializing with their superiors outside of work. I also told him/her that we take this policy very seriously because it can harm our relationship with our customers and suppliers. If he/she violates this policy in the future, he/she will be subject to discipline, up to and including termination of employment.

(Solution) - The employee will be required to attend a meeting with me within _____ days to discuss this matter. If he/she does not attend this meeting voluntarily, disciplinary action may be taken against him/her, up to and including termination of employment.

Approved By: Date

Manager Signature and Title

82. Sabotaging Coworkers

Use the following template for violation of company policy on sabotaging coworker:

Date

Employee Name

(Problem Relevance) Violation of policy for attempting to sabotage coworkers.

(Problem Cause) The cause of the employee's violation is found to be general disdain.

(Problem Analysis) On [date], I observed the employee delete a co-worker's work files while in the break room.

(Action Taken) I have advised the employee that it is our policy to prohibit employees from sabotaging other employees. In addition, I have reminded him/her that we take our policy regarding workplace violence very seriously. If he/she does not follow this policy in the future, he/she will be subject to discipline up to and including termination of employment.

(Solution) The employee will be required to attend a meeting with me within _____ days to discuss this matter. If he/she does not attend this meeting voluntarily, disciplinary action may be taken against him/her, up to and including termination of employment.

Approved By: Date

Manager Signature and Title

Chapter 6: General Attendance Problems

In this chapter, we will provide you with sample write-ups to deal with different attendance and tardiness problems. Attendance is critical to the success of any company or organization. A company that produces quality products needs employees who are on time and dependable. An employee who is tardy, absent from work without notice, or has frequent unexcused absences has a negative impact on the productivity of the department and organization as a whole.

Attendance problems also impact the company's bottom line. According to the U.S. Department of Labor, it costs an employer $300 for every hour an employee is absent from work. This figure includes wages and benefits that are paid to employees who are absent from work, as well as administrative costs such as advertising for replacements and making up for work not accomplished while an employee was absent from work.

Let's take a look at the sample write-up below and see how the section headings "Problem," "Summary," and "Action" work to provide the facts of a problem.

83. Misusing Sick Leave for Personal Vacation

Some employees may misuse sick leave for personal vacation. In this type of situation, the employee may take a few days off from work to go on vacation, even though he/she does not have an illness or injury that prevents him/her from working. Use the following template for violation of company policy on misusing sick leave for personal vacation:

Date

Employee Name

(Problem Relevance) - Violation of Company Policy on Misusing Sick Leave for Personal Vacation.

(Problem Cause) The cause of the employee's violation is due to his/her abuse of sick leave.

(Problem Analysis) - On [date], I observed the employee leaving work at [time] even though he/she did not have a doctor's note. In addition, I observed him/her boarding a flight to [destination] at [time] on that same day.

(Action Taken) - I advised the employee that we have a strict policy against employees abusing sick leave to take days off from work and still be paid their full salary. In addition, I told him/her that we take this policy very seriously because it affects our bottom line. If he/she violates this policy in the future, he/she will be subject to discipline, up to and including termination of employment.

(Solution) - The employee will be required to attend a meeting with me within _____ days to discuss this matter. If he/she does not attend this meeting voluntarily, disciplinary action may be taken against him/her, up to and including termination of employment.

Approved By: Date

Manager Signature and Title

84. False Claim of Illness

Employees who call in sick when they are not actually ill may be trying to avoid work. This is a violation of company policy, and may also violate state law. Use the following template for violation of company policy on false claim of illness:

Date

Employee Name

(Problem Relevance) - Violation of Company Policy on False Claim of Illness.

(Problem Cause) - The cause of the employee's violation is bad outlook.

(Problem Analysis) - On [date], I received a call from the employee stating that he/she would be unable to work today because he/she is ill. However, when I telephoned his/her home at [time], I learned that he/she had left the house and gone elsewhere. In addition, I have received reports that the employee has called in sick when he or she was not actually ill on the following dates: [list dates].

(Action Taken) - I have advised the employee that it is our policy to prohibit employees from falsely claiming to be sick. In addition, I have reminded him/her that we take our policy regarding false claims very seriously. If he/she does not follow this policy in the future, he/she will be subject to discipline, up to and including termination of employment.

(Solution) - The employee will be required to attend a meeting with me within _____ days to discuss this matter. If he/she does not attend this meeting voluntarily, disciplinary action may be taken against him/her, up to and including termination of employment.

Approved By: Date

Manager Signature and Title

85. Absences Without Approved Leave

Absences without approved leave may be a sign of potential impairment on the part of the employee. If the employee is experiencing problems at home or with a medical condition that is causing the absences, you should find out about these issues before taking any disciplinary action. Use the following template for violation of company policy on absences without approved leave:

Date

Employee Name

(Problem Relevance) - Violation of Company Policy on Absences Without Approved Leave.
(Problem cause) – The cause was deemed to be a callous attitude.
(Action Taken) - I have told the employee that it is our policy to require employees to obtain approval from their supervisors prior to taking an absence from work. In addition, I have reminded him/her that we take our policy regarding absences very seriously. If he/she does not follow this policy in the future, he/she will be subject to discipline, up to and including termination of employment.
(Solution) - The employee will be required to attend a meeting with me within _____ days to discuss this matter. If he/she does not attend this meeting voluntarily, disciplinary action may be taken against him/her, up to and including termination of employment.

Approved By: Date

Manager Signature and Title

86. Repeated Inadequate Explanations for Absences

The definition of "inadequate" explanations for absences varies depending on the situation. Generally, however, an employee should not make excuses that are inconsistent with other facts or circumstances or that are unrealistic or unreasonable. In addition, the employee should not make excuses that are contrary to established policies and procedures. Use the following template for violation of company policy on repeated inadequate explanations for absence:

Date

Employee Name

(Problem Relevance) - Repeated Inadequate Explanations for Absences.

(Problem Cause) - The cause of the employee's violation is misusing excuses.

(Problem Analysis) - On [date], the employee was late for work. He/she informed me that he/she was late because he/she overslept. In addition, I have received reports that the employee has been absent from work five times during each of the past three calendar years and has provided unacceptable explanations for those absences.

(Action Taken) - I advised the employee that it is our policy to require employees to provide acceptable explanations for their absences. In addition, I have reminded him/her that we take our policy regarding repeated inadequate explanations for absences very seriously. If he/she does not follow this policy in the future, he/she will be subject to discipline, up to and including termination of employment.

(Solution) - The employee will be required to attend a meeting with me within _____ days to discuss this matter. If he/she does not attend this meeting voluntarily, disciplinary

action may be taken against him/her, up to and including termination of employment.

Approved By: Date

Manager Signature and Title

87. Failure to Report on Time

On time reporting to work is an important part of employee performance. When employees report to work late without good reason, they are not following their employer's rules. This violates the company's policy on punctuality. Use the following template for violation of company policy on failure to report:

Date

Employee Name

(Problem Relevance) - Violation of Company Policy on Failure to Report on Time.
(Problem Cause) The cause of the employee's violation is due to the employee's failure to follow a rule.
(Problem Analysis) - On [date], I observed the employee arrive at work at [time]. When asked why he/she was late, he/she said that he/she forgot to set his/her alarm clock.
(Action Taken) - I advised the employee that we have a strict policy against employees who arrive at work late without good reason. In addition, I told him/her that we take our policies regarding failure to report on time very seriously. If he/she violates this policy in the future, he/she will be subject to discipline, up to and including termination of employment.
(Solution) - The employee will be required to attend a meeting with me within _____ days to discuss this matter. If

he/she does not attend this meeting voluntarily, disciplinary action may be taken against him/her, up to and including termination of employment.

Approved By: Date

Manager Signature and Title

88. Blaming Others for Failure

In cases where an employee has committed a violation of the company's rules, the employee may attempt to blame someone else for this violation. The employee may also try to shift the blame to another person by presenting false or misleading information. Use the following template for violation of company policy on blaming others:

Date

Employee Name

(Problem Relevance) - Violation of Company Policy on Blaming Others for Failure.
(Problem Cause) The cause of the employee's violation is due to his/her attempt to shift responsibility for failure onto someone else.
(Problem Analysis) - On [date], I observed the employee violate company policy by failing to report on time. When asked why he/she was late, he/she said that his/her supervisor did not give him/her enough time to prepare for the meeting.
(Action Taken) - I advised the employee that we have a strict policy against employees who attempt to shift responsibility for failure onto someone else. In addition, I told him/her that we take our policies regarding failure very seriously. If he/she

violates this policy in the future, he/she will be subject to discipline, up to and including termination of employment.

(Solution) - The employee will be required to attend a meeting with me within _____ days to discuss this matter. If he/she does not attend this meeting voluntarily, disciplinary action may be taken against him/her, up to and including termination of employment.

(Follow Up) If the employee violates this policy again, he/she will be subject to discipline, up to and including termination of employment.

Approved By: Date

Manager Signature and Title

Chapter 7: Immediate Termination

Immediate termination is the next step in progressive discipline.

It is a serious action that should be taken only when other forms of discipline have been unsuccessful. When immediate termination is necessary, it should be done with sensitivity and compassion. The supervisor should outline the reasons for the action and attempt to outline potential career opportunities.

The supervisor should consider the need to sustain morale and maintain a positive relationship with the employee. Above all, he or she must be professional in carrying out the termination. Immediate termination is rarely a wise course of action. It is an extreme action that should be used only when there is no alternative if serious offenses have been committed, and when other forms of discipline have been unsuccessful. It is important to remember that the decision to terminate an employee is a serious one.

Immediate termination should not be used to punish employees for minor offenses, or for those who make mistakes in the workplace. This action should be reserved only for serious violations of company policies and procedures. It should be used only as a last resort after all other forms of discipline have failed. The following are some examples of circumstances that might warrant immediate termination:

89. Commercial Espionage

Commercial espionage is the obtaining of secret, confidential or proprietary information of a business competitor for the purpose of giving an unfair competitive advantage. It is a form of theft and is subject to criminal prosecution. Employees should be aware that there are severe consequences if they engage in commercial espionage. Use the following template for violation of company policy on commercial espionage:

Date

Employee Name

(Problem Relevance) - Violation of Company Policy on Commercial Espionage.
(Problem Cause) The cause of the employee's violation is due to the employee's desire to gain an advantage over his/her employer.
(Problem Analysis) - On [date], I observed the employee copying documents from our files at [time]. I asked him/her why he/she was copying these documents, and he/she said that he/she is planning to use the information for a project at his/her new job.
(Action Taken) - I advised the employee that we have a strict policy against employees copying company materials or documents without permission. In addition, I told him/her that we take this policy very seriously because it directly affects our profits. If he/she violates this policy in the future, he/she will be subject to discipline up to and including termination of employment.
(Solution) - The employee will be required to attend a meeting with me within _____ days to discuss this matter. If he/she does not attend this meeting voluntarily, disciplinary action may be taken against him/her, up to and including termination of employment.

Approved By: Date

Manager Signature and Title

90. Blackmail

Blackmail is an attempt to obtain something from another person by threatening to harm that person or someone they care about. Examples of blackmail include:

- Stealing money or trade secrets and then threatening to disclose the information if you are not paid a ransom.
- Intimidating or harassing someone with the intent of receiving money, property, or any other thing of value.
- Using material (such as slander) about a person that will affect their ability to get or keep a job, credit, etc.

An employee may sometimes use threats of embarrassment or harassment to gain something. For example, an employee may threaten to tell a coworker that he/she is failing a class if the coworker does not help the employee with a task, such as grading papers for a class. Use the following template for violation of company policy on blackmail:

Date

Employee Name

(Problem Relevance) - Violation of Company Policy on Blackmail.
(Problem Cause) The cause of the employee's violation is due to his/her desire to gain something.
(Problem Analysis) - On [date], I observed the employee threatening to tell another coworker that he/she is failing a class if the coworker does not help the employee with the grading of papers for a class.

(Action Taken) - I advised the employee that we have a strict policy against employees who use threats of embarrassment or harassment to gain something. In addition, I told him/her that we take our policies regarding blackmail with harassment very seriously because such actions are not acceptable for people in the professional world. If he/she violates this policy in the future, he/she will be subject to discipline, up to and including termination of employment.

(Solution) - The employee will be required to attend a meeting with me within _____ days to discuss this matter. If he/she does not attend this meeting voluntarily, disciplinary action may be taken against him/her, up to and including termination of employment.

Approved By: Date

Manager Signature and Title

91. Breach of Contract

An employee's failure to perform a contract with his/her employer may result in disciplinary action against the employee. The employee may be terminated if he/she breaches the contract on more than one occasion. Use the following template for violation of company policy on breach of contract:

Date

Employee Name

(Problem Relevance) - Violation of Company Policy on Breach of Contract.
(Problem Cause) The cause of the employee's violation is due to his/her failure to perform a contractual obligation.

(Problem Analysis) - On [date], I observed the employee breach the company's contract with [name] by failing to deliver [product or service]. He/she failed to deliver this product or service on [date].

(Action Taken) - I advised the employee that we have a strict policy against employees who fail to perform their contractual obligations. In addition, I told him/her that we take our policies regarding breach of contract very seriously. If he/she violates this policy in the future, he/she will be subject to discipline, up to and including termination of employment.

(Solution) - The employee will be required to attend a meeting with me within _____ days to discuss this matter. If he/she does not attend this meeting voluntarily, disciplinary action may be taken against him/her, up to and including termination of employment.

Approved By: Date

Manager Signature and Title

92. Conviction for Crimes

Employees are expected to respect the rights of others. Therefore, an employee may be disciplined for committing a crime that violates these rights. Use the following template for violation of company policy on conviction for crimes:

Date

Employee Name

(Problem Relevance) - Violation of Company Policy on Conviction for Crimes.

(Problem Cause) The cause of the employee's violation is due to the employee's conviction for crimes.

(Problem Analysis) - On [date], I received a copy of the court record showing that the employee pled guilty to [crime].

(Action Taken) - I advised the employee that we have a strict policy against employees who commit crimes. In addition, I told him/her that we take this policy very seriously because it directly affects our reputation. If he/she violates this policy in the future, he/she will be subject to discipline, up to and including termination of employment.

(Solution) - The employee will be required to attend a meeting with me within _____ days to discuss this matter. If he/she does not attend this meeting voluntarily, disciplinary action may be taken against him/her, up to and including termination of employment.

Approved By: Date

Manager Signature and Title

93. Threatening to Harm Her/Himself

In some cases, an employee may threaten to harm himself/herself. This presents a problem for the employer because the employee continues to work while making such threats. Yet the employee's threats are a violation of company policy. Use the following template for violation of company policy on threatening to self-harm:

Date

Employee Name

(Problem Relevance) - Violation of Company Policy on Threatening to Self-Harm.

(Problem Cause) The cause of the employee's violation is due to the employee's concern about his/her mental health.

(Problem Analysis) - On [date], I received a phone call from [name] who is related to the employee. [Name] told me that the employee is threatening to harm himself/herself.

(Action Taken) - I advised [name] to inform the employee's supervisor immediately about his/her mental health condition.

(Solution) - The employee will be required to attend a meeting with me within _____ days to discuss this matter. If he/she does not attend this meeting voluntarily, disciplinary action may be taken against him/her, up to and including termination of employment.

Approved By: Date

Manager Signature and Title

94. Providing False Information in Job Application

Employees who provide false information in a job application or on a job application form are violating company policy. This type of violation of company policy may be grounds for termination because it is fraudulent. Use the following template for violation of company policy on providing false information in a job application:

Date

Employee Name

(Problem Relevance) - Violation of Company Policy on Providing False Information in a Job Application.

(Problem Cause) The cause of the employee's violation is due to the employee's false statement in his/her job application or on a job application form.

(Problem Analysis) - On [date], while reviewing the employee's job application, I discovered that he/she listed the following information on his/her job application:

(Action Taken) - I advised the employee that we have a strict policy against falsifying information in a job application or on a job application form. In addition, I told him/her that we take our policies regarding providing false information in a job application very seriously. If he/she violates this policy in the future, he/she will be subject to discipline, up to and including termination of employment.

(Solution) - The employee will be required to attend a meeting with me within _____ days to discuss this matter. If he/she does not attend this meeting voluntarily, disciplinary action may be taken against him/her, up to and including termination of employment.

Approved By: Date

Manager Signature and Title

95. Working on Multiple Jobs in the Workplace

Some employers permit employees to work on multiple jobs in the workplace. This can result in poor work quality and can sometimes cause a conflict of interest. For instance, an employee may be working on a project for the company while also working on his/her own personal project (such as sales of used items) at the same time. Use the following template for violation of company policy on working on multiple jobs in the workplace:

Date

Employee Name

(Problem Relevance) - Violation of Company Policy on Working on Multiple Jobs in the Workplace.

(Problem Cause) The cause of the employee's violation is due to conflict of interest.

(Problem Analysis) - On [date], I observed the employee working on more than one job in the workplace. This is a violation of our policy on working on multiple jobs in the workplace.

(Action Taken) - I advised the employee that we have a strict policy against employees who work on multiple jobs in the workplace. In addition, I told him/her that we take this policy very seriously because it directly affects our profits. If he/she violates this policy in the future, he/she will be subject to discipline, up to and including termination of employment.

(Solution) - The employee will be required to attend a meeting with me within _____ days to discuss this matter. If he/she does not attend this meeting voluntarily, disciplinary action may be taken against him/her, up to and including termination of employment.

Approved By: Date

Manager Signature and Title

96. Inviting Unauthorized Personnel to Workplace

When an employee invites unauthorized personnel to his/her workplace, the employee may be violating the company's policy on unauthorized personnel in workplace. Use the following template for violation of company policy on inviting unauthorized personnel to workplace:

Date

Employee Name

(Problem Relevance) - Violation of Company Policy on Inviting Unauthorized Personnel to Workplace.

(Problem Cause) The cause of the employee's violation is due to the employee's failure to follow a rule.

(Problem Analysis) - On [date], I observed the employee talking with a person at [location]. When asked about this person, he/she said that it was his/her friend and that he/she invited him/her to the workplace.

(Action Taken) - I advised the employee that we have a strict policy against employees who invite unauthorized personnel to our workplace. In addition, I told him/her that we take this policy very seriously because it affects our security and confidentiality policies. If he/she violates this policy in the future, he/she will be subject to discipline, up to and including termination of employment.

(Solution) - The employee will be required to attend a meeting with me within _____ days to discuss this matter. If he/she does not attend this meeting voluntarily, disciplinary action may be taken against him/her, up to and including termination of employment.

Approved By: Date

Manager Signature and Title

97. Endangering Coworkers

Employees have a duty to ensure that they do not endanger their coworkers. In some cases, employees may endanger the lives of their coworkers by engaging in activities that are prohibited by company policy or a safety regulation. In other cases, employees may engage in activities that are permitted by company policy or a safety regulation, but they do so in such a way that they endanger the lives of their coworkers. Use the following template for violation of company policy on endangering coworkers:

Date

Employee Name

(Problem Relevance) - Violation of Company Policy on Endangering Coworkers.

(Problem Cause) The cause of the employee's violation is due to the employee's failure to follow a rule.

(Problem Analysis) - On [date], I observed the employee [activity]. When I questioned him/her about this activity, he/she said that he/she thought it was okay because it is permitted by our company's policy. However, he/she did not realize that his/her action placed the lives of his/her coworkers in danger.

(Action Taken) - I advised the employee that we have a strict policy against employees who engage in activities that endanger the lives of their coworkers. In addition, I told him/her that we take this policy very seriously because it directly affects our profits and our reputation as a business. If he/she violates this policy in the future, he/she will be subject to discipline, up to and including termination of employment.

(Solution) - The employee will be required to attend a meeting with me within _____ days to discuss this matter. If he/she does not attend this meeting voluntarily, disciplinary action may be taken against him/her, up to and including termination of employment.

Approved By: Date

Manager Signature and Title

98. Workplace Segregation

Race, gender, and age discrimination are all prohibited by Title VII of the Civil Rights Act of 1964, which is enforced by the Equal Employment Opportunity Commission (EEOC). Some states have their own laws prohibiting these forms of workplace discrimination. These laws do not just apply to new hires, but to all employees. The law is intended to protect employees from being treated differently because of a personal characteristic that does not affect job performance (e.g., race, sex, age). Use the following template for violation of company policy on workplace segregation:

Date

Employee Name

(Problem Relevance) - Violation of Company Policy on Workplace Segregation.
(Problem Cause) The cause of the employee's violation is due to the employee's failure to follow a rule.
(Problem Analysis) - On [date], I observed the employee speaking with a company employee insensitively at an off-site meeting. The company employee is white, and the employee is black.
(Action Taken) - I advised the employee that we have a strict policy against insensitive or racial conversations at work if employees are of different races or of different genders. In addition, I told him/her that we take our policies regarding workplace segregation very seriously because it directly affects our profits. If he/she violates this policy in the future, he/she

will be subject to discipline, up to and including termination of employment.

(Solution) - The employee will be required to attend a meeting with me within _____ days to discuss this matter. If he/she does not attend this meeting voluntarily, disciplinary action may be taken against him/her, up to and including termination of employment.

Approved By: Date

Manager Signature and Title

99. Bullying Coworkers into Forced Work

Some employers have a policy against coworkers who force other employees to work. This is not permissible because it violates the employees' right to decide whether or not they want to work. Use the following template for violation of company policy on bullying coworkers into forced work:

Date

Employee Name

(Problem Relevance) - Violation of Company Policy on Bullying Coworkers into Forced Work.
(Problem Cause) The cause of the employee's violation is due to his/her failure to follow an employer rule.
(Problem Analysis) - On [date], I observed the employee pressuring another coworker into working on a Saturday when the coworker did not want to do so. When asked why he/she was pressuring him/her into working, the employee said that he/she had to work on Saturday because he/she did not want to be fired.

(Action Taken) - I advised the employee that we have a strict policy against coworkers who pressure other coworkers into working. In addition, I told him/her that we take our policies regarding bullying coworkers into forced work very seriously and that if he/she violates this policy in the future, he/she will be subject to discipline, up to and including termination of employment.

(Solution) - The employee will be required to attend a meeting with me within _____ days to discuss this matter. If he/she does not attend this meeting voluntarily, disciplinary action may be taken against him/her, up to and including termination of employment.

Approved By: Date

Manager Signature and Title

100. Forgery

Forgery is the unauthorized use of another person's signature. This can be done by anyone, including employees, customers, vendors, and competitors. Use the following template for violation of company policy on forgery:

Date

Employee Name

(Problem Relevance) - Violation of Company Policy on Forgery.

(Problem Cause) The cause of the employee's violation is due to his/her unauthorized use of another person's signature.

(Problem Analysis) - On [date], I was examining our shipping documents and found that they indicated that a shipment was received from [company]. However, when I contacted [company], they said that they did not receive this shipment. The shipment was received at [time] on [date].

(Action Taken) - I advised the employee that we have a strict policy against employees who forge another person's signature. In addition, I told him/her that we take this policy very seriously because it directly affects our profits. If he/she violates this policy in the future, he/she will be subject to discipline, up to and including termination of employment.

(Solution) - The employee will be required to attend a meeting with me within _____ days to discuss this matter. If he/she does not attend this meeting voluntarily, disciplinary action may be taken against him/her, up to and including termination of employment.

Approved By: Date

Manager Signature and Title

101. Hiding or Destroying Evidence of Wrongdoing

Some employees attempt to hide or destroy evidence of their wrongdoing. In some cases, they may arrive at work early to remove incriminating information. In other cases, they may use the company's computers or phones to send an e-mail or make a telephone call that would cause trouble for them if it were discovered by their supervisor.

Solicitation on behalf of a third-party is usually considered a form of financial fraud on the employer. This type of solicitation can involve any person who attempts to sell products or services to an employer on behalf of a third-party. For example, an employee may try to sell goods or services to his/her employer without disclosing that he/she is doing so on behalf of a third-party. As another example, an employee may try to sell his/her employer items that he/she received as gifts from a third-party. Use the following template for violation of company policy on hiding or destroying evidence:

Date

Employee Name

(Problem Relevance) - Violation of Company Policy on Hiding or Destroying Evidence.

(Problem Cause) The cause of the employee's violation is due to blackmail.

(Problem Analysis) - On [date], I observed the employee arriving for work at [time] while sending an email on our company computer. The subject line of the email was "Wedding photos," and the employee was using the computer in his/her area to send the email.

(Action Taken) - I advised the employee that we have a strict policy against employees using company computers or phones to send any personal messages. In addition, I told him/her that we take our policies regarding hiding or destroying evidence very seriously. If he/she violates this policy in the future, he/she will be subject to discipline, up to and including termination of employment.

(Solution) - The employee will be required to attend a meeting with me within _____ days to discuss this matter. If he/she does not attend this meeting voluntarily, disciplinary action may be taken against him/her, up to and including termination of employment.

Approved By: Date

Manager Signature and Title

102. Embezzling Company Funds

Embezzlement is the act of stealing money or property that is owned by a company. Employers have a responsibility to protect their companies' assets from theft and embezzlement. A person who embezzles money or property owns up to his/her actions. That means he/she takes responsibility for the theft or embezzlement, and he/she agrees to pay the amount of money or property back. The person who embezzled is no longer considered an employee of the company. He/she is now a thief, and he/she is treated like a criminal because stealing company money or property is a crime. Use the following template for violation of company policy on embezzling company funds:

Date

Employee Name

(Problem Relevance) - Embezzling Company Funds.
(Problem Cause) The cause of the employee's violation is due to blackmail.
(Problem Analysis) - On [date], I observed the employee purchasing a [item] online using our company credit card. The [item] was delivered to his/her home address on that same day.
(Action Taken) - I advised the employee that we have a strict policy against employees using company credit cards for personal purchases on the Internet. In addition, I told him/her that we take our policies regarding embezzlement very seriously. If he/she violates this policy in the future, he/she will be subject to discipline, up to and including termination of employment.
(Solution) - The employee will be required to pay back the money spent on the [item] by [date]. If he/she does not pay back this money by that date, disciplinary action may be taken

against him/her, up to and including termination of employment.

Approved By: Date

Manager Signature and Title

103. Providing False Business Records

Employees are sometimes required to submit certain records to comply with company policy, taxation requirements, or government regulations. In some cases, employees may falsely record or report information on these records to avoid following company policies or making their superiors look bad. Use the following template for violation of company policy on providing false business records:

Date

Employee Name

(Problem Relevance) - Violation of Company Policy on Providing False Business Records.
(Problem Cause) The cause of the employee's violation is due to the employee's failure to follow a rule.
(Problem Analysis) - On [date], I observed the employee submit false information on a [record name] required by the company. The record was submitted at [time] on [date].
(Action Taken) - I advised the employee that we have a strict policy against employees who submit false information on business records required by the company. In addition, I told him/her that we take this policy very seriously because it directly affects our taxes and the way in which our superiors view us. If he/she violates this policy in the future, he/she will

be subject to discipline, up to and including termination of employment.

(Solution) - The employee will be required to attend a meeting with me within _____ days to discuss this matter. If he/she does not attend this meeting voluntarily, disciplinary action may be taken against him/her, up to and including termination of employment.

Approved By: Date

Manager Signature and Title

104. Perpetrating Financial Fraud on the Employer

Employees who engage in financial fraud against their employers can cause significant financial harm to the employer. This type of fraud can be perpetrated by employees who have access to assets and funds owned by the employer. Once an employee has engaged in this type of fraud, it can be difficult and time consuming for the employer to recover any losses caused by the employee's fraudulent conduct.

Employees who perpetrate financial fraud on their employers often do so because they believe they can make significant amounts of money doing so or because they believe that they can get away with it without being caught. Therefore, you should take appropriate actions to prevent financial fraud on your organization. For example, you should ensure that all employees who have access to your assets and funds are thoroughly screened before you hire them.

Employees who perpetrate financial fraud may resign quickly, transfer to another location, or even leave the organization. They also may attempt to cover up their misdeeds by falsifying documents or destroying incriminating evidence. As a result, it is often very important for you to document your actions regarding employees who are suspected or known to be perpetrating financial fraud on their employers. To help you enforce your policies regarding financial fraud, use the following template:

Date

Employee Name

(Problem Relevance) - Violation of Company Policy on Financial Fraud.

(Problem Cause) - The cause of the violation is due to financial gains.

(Problem Analysis) - On [date], I received a report from [source] that the employee had misappropriated funds from our accounts. On [date], I also observed the employee entering inaccurate information in our computer system. On [date], I observed him/her recording incorrect information in our inventory database. In addition, on [date], I checked our accounts payable records and found that they contained numerous discrepancies caused by the employee.

(Action Taken) - I have advised the employee that he/she is not to access any areas of our computer system, accounts payable files, or inventory records without my permission. If he/she does not follow this policy in the future, he/she will be subject to disciplinary action and up to and including termination of employment.

(Solution) - The employee will be required to attend a meeting with me within _____ days to discuss this matter. If he/she does not attend this meeting voluntarily, disciplinary action may be taken against him/her, up to and including termination of employment.

Approved By: Date

Manager Signature and Title

Chapter 8: Miscellaneous Problems

You may have some other problems with an employee that are not covered in the preceding discussion. These problems may be unique to the employee or unique to your organization. There are no hard and fast rules for handling these problems, but there are some guidelines that may help you. The following are suggestions only and do not cover all types of problems. Let's look at some of the problems that may not be covered in the preceding discussion.

105. Interferes with Employee's Work Progress

Interfering with an employee's work progress is a violation of company policy. All employees should respect others and not let their personal feelings interfere with an employee's work. Use the following template for violation of company policy on interfering with another employee's work progress:

Date

Employee Name

(Problem Relevance) - Violation of Company Policy on Interferes with Employee's Work Progress.
(Problem Cause) The cause of the employee's violation is due to his/her personal feelings affecting his/her conduct at work.
(Problem Analysis) - On [date], I observed the employee [describe what was observed]. He/she said that he/she was fed up with [name] because [describe what the employee said].
(Action Taken) - I advised the employee that we have a strict policy against employees who interfere with their co-workers' work progress. In addition, I told him/her that we take our

policies regarding interference with an employee's work progress very seriously. If he/she violates this policy in the future, he/she will be subject to discipline, up to and including termination of employment.

(Solution) - The employee will be required to attend a meeting with me within _____ days to discuss this matter. If he/she does not attend this meeting voluntarily, disciplinary action may be taken against him/her, up to and including termination of employment.

Approved By: Date

Manager Signature and Title

106. Instigating Riots in the Workplace

While some conflict among employees is normal, situations may arise in which one or more employees raise the level of conflict, often to a disruptive level. This happens when one or more employees instigate riots in the workplace. Such an employee(s) may intentionally create and escalate conflicts using verbal abuse, threats of physical violence, or actual violence. Use the following template for violation of company policy on instigates riots in the workplace:

Date

Employee Name

(Problem Relevance) - Violation of Company Policy on Instigating Riots in the Workplace.
(Problem Cause) The cause of the employee's violation is due to inappropriate behavior such as verbal abuse or threatening physical violence.

(Problem Analysis) - On [date], I observed the employee threaten to hit another employee. He/she made this threat at a staff meeting on [date] at [time].

(Action Taken) - I advised the employee that threatening physical violence is inappropriate behavior in the workplace and is a violation of our company's policy on instigating riots in the workplace. In addition, I told him/her that we take this policy very seriously because it directly affects our productivity. If he/she threatens physical violence in the future, he/she will be subject to discipline, up to and including termination of employment.

(Solution) - The employee will be required to attend a meeting with me within _____ days to discuss this matter. If he/she does not attend this meeting voluntarily, disciplinary action may be taken against him/her, up to and including termination of employment.

Approved By: Date

Manager Signature and Title

107. Invading Coworkers Private Space

In some companies, employees are allowed to store personal items in their desk or locker. However, when an employee begins to store items in his/her coworker's desk or locker, the problem becomes more complicated. When an employee begins to abuse this privilege by storing items that belong to him/her in a coworker's desk or locker (without the coworker's permission), it violates company policy on invasion of a coworker's private space. Use the following template for violation of company policy on invasion of a coworker's private space:

Date

Employee Name

(Problem Relevance) - Violation of Company Policy on Invasion of Coworkers Private Space.

(Problem Cause) The cause of the employee's violation is due to the employee's failure to follow a rule.

(Problem Analysis) - On [date], I observed the employee storing his/her personal items in his/her coworker's desk on [date]. When asked why he/she was storing his/her personal items in another employee's desk, he/she said that he/she wanted to keep some of his/her personal items at work because it would be easier than going home and then coming back to work.

(Action Taken) - I advised the employee that we have a strict policy against employees who invade their coworker's private space. In addition, I told him/her that we take our policies regarding invasion of a coworker's private space very seriously because it is an invasion of the coworker's privacy. If he/she violates this policy in the future, he/she will be subject to discipline, up to and including termination of employment.

(Solution) - The employee will be required to attend a meeting with me within _____ days to discuss this matter. If he/she does not attend this meeting voluntarily, disciplinary action may be taken against him/her, up to and including termination of employment.

Approved By: Date

Manager Signature and Title

108. Falsifying Sexual Harassment

In some cases, an employee may falsify sexual harassment to get out of work or to gain some other advantage. For example, an employee may claim that a supervisor sexually harassed him/her when in fact the employee was not harassed. Use the following template for violation of company policy on falsifying sexual harassment:

Date

Employee Name

(Problem Relevance) - Violation of Company Policy on Falsifying Sexual Harassment.

(Problem Cause) The cause of the employee's violation is due to the employee's desire to evade work responsibilities and/or to gain an advantage.

(Problem Analysis) - On [date], I advised the employee that he/she will need to fill out a form indicating whether or not he/she feels that he/she has been sexually harassed. When asked why the employee replied that he/she felt sexually harassed by his/her supervisor. However, he/she did not fill out a form indicating whether or not he/she was sexually harassed.

(Action Taken) - I told him/her that we take our sexual harassment policy very seriously because we need to know if any of our employees are being sexually harassed to prevent it. If he/she does not fill out the form indicating whether or not he/she felt sexually harassed within the next _____ days, disciplinary action may be taken against him/her, up to and including termination of employment.

(Solution) - The employee will be required to fill out a form indicating whether or not he/she felt sexually harassed within the next _____ days. If he/she does not fill out the form voluntarily, I will give him/her the forms and then have him/her sign them.

Approved By: Date

Manager Signature and Title

109. Refusal to Listen to Warnings

Employees should listen to warnings from their employers. When employees do not listen to their employers' warnings, they may be fired. Use the following template for violation of company policy on refusing to listen to warning:

Date

Employee Name

(Problem Relevance) - Violation of Company Policy on Refusing to Listen to Warnings.
(Problem Cause) The cause of the employee's violation is due to the employee's failure/refusal to follow a rule.
(Problem Analysis) - On [date], I warned the employee that he/she would be fired if he/she repeated his/her unacceptable behavior. Nonetheless, I observed him/her repeating this behavior today at [time].
(Action Taken) - I fired the employee for repeated violation of our company's policy.

Approved By: Date

Manager Signature and Title

110. Inappropriate Relationship with Clients

Employees may have to meet with clients on occasion. There are rules against having a relationship with a client that would be inappropriate for an employee. Use the following template for violation of company policy on inappropriate relationship with clients:

Date

Employee Name

(Problem Relevance) - Violation of Company Policy on Inappropriate Relationship with Clients.

(Problem Cause) The cause of the employee's violation is due to the employee's inappropriate relationship with a client.

(Problem Analysis) - On [date], I observed the employee meeting privately in his/her office with one of our clients. He/she was alone in his/her office. When I asked the employee what he/she was doing in his/her office, he/she said that they were discussing an upcoming project for their company. I informed the employee that we have a strict policy against employees having private meetings with clients, because it could lead to an inappropriate relationship with a client. In addition, I told him/her that we take this policy very seriously because it directly affects our profits. If he/she violates this policy in the future, he/she will be subject to discipline, up to and including termination of employment.

(Solution) - The employee will be required to attend a meeting with me within _____ days to discuss this matter. If he/she does not attend this meeting voluntarily, disciplinary action may be taken against him/her, up to and including termination of employment.

Approved By: Date

Manager Signature and Title

111. Public Display of Affection in Workplace

Public displays of affection in the workplace are not acceptable. Some companies have policies against public displays of affection for this reason. Use the following template for violation of company policy:

Date

Employee Name

(Problem Relevance) - Violation of Company Policy on Public Display of Affection in the Workplace.

(Problem Cause) The cause of this employee's violation is due to the employee's public display of affection.

(Problem Analysis) - On [date], I observed the employee engaging in a public display of affection with his/her significant other at [time] on [date].

(Action Taken) - I advised the employee that such behavior is unacceptable in our workplace and that if he/she does it again, he/she will be subject to disciplinary action, up to and including termination of employment.

(Solution) - The employee will be required to attend a meeting with me within _____ days to discuss this matter. If he/she does not attend this meeting voluntarily, disciplinary action may be taken against him/her, up to and including termination of employment.

Approved By: Date

Manager Signature and Title

112. Using Workplace Authority for Personal Gain

Sometimes an employee may use his/her position to benefit himself/herself rather than for the benefit of the company. This violates the company's policy on authority abuse. Use the following template for violation of company policy on authority abuse:

Date

Employee Name

(Problem Relevance) - Violation of Company Policy on Authority Abuse.

(Problem Cause) The cause of the employee's violation is due to the employee's abuse of his/her workplace authority.

(Problem Analysis) - On [date], I observed the employee abusing his/her power by giving away free tickets to another employee even though such action was contrary to a previous agreement between them that he/she would buy the tickets for the other employee. The tickets were given away on [date] at [time].

(Action Taken) - I advised the employee that we have a strict policy against employees who abuse their workplace authority by giving away free tickets to another employee even though such action was contrary to a previous agreement between them that he/she would buy the tickets for the other employee. In addition, I told him/her that we take our policies regarding abuse of workplace authority very seriously because such actions may result in harm to the company's profits. If he/she violates this policy in the future, he/she will be subject to discipline, up to and including termination of employment.

(Solution) - The employee will be required to attend a meeting with me within _____ days to discuss this matter. If he/she does not attend this meeting voluntarily, disciplinary

action may be taken against him/her, up to and including termination of employment.

Approved By: Date

Manager Signature and Title

113. Damaging Company Owned Property

Some employees may be careless and fail to take care of company property. This may lead them to damage company property. In addition, some employees may damage property when they try to repair it or make it work. They do not follow the rules and regulations of the company in this regard. This violates the company's policy on damaging company owned property. Use the following template for violation of company policy on damaging company owned property:

Date

Employee Name

(Problem Relevance) - Violation of Company Policy on Damaging Company Owned Property.
(Problem Cause) The cause of the employee's violation is due to his/her carelessness.
(Problem Analysis) - On [date], I observed the employee damage [name of machine or item] by [describe how it was damaged].
(Action Taken) - I advised the employee that we take our company's property very seriously and that we expect him/her to take care of it. In addition, I told him/her that we have a strict policy against employees damaging company property. If he/she does so in the future, he/she will be subject to discipline, up to and including termination of employment.

(Solution) - The employee will be required to attend a meeting with me within _____ days to discuss this matter. If he/she does not attend this meeting voluntarily, disciplinary action may be taken against him/her, up to and including termination of employment.

Approved By: Date

Manager Signature and Title

114. Persistent Negativity

Employees who are constantly negative about their work and coworkers may also be violating company policy. Negativity reflects a lack of commitment to the workplace and to other employees. Use the following template for violation of company policy on persistent negativity:

Date

Employee Name

(Problem Relevance) - Violation of Company Policy on Persistent Negativity.
(Problem Cause) The cause of the employee's violation is due to his/her negative attitude regarding his/her work or coworkers.
(Problem Analysis) - On [date], I observed the employee complaining about his/her coworker during my conversation with him/her. When asked why he/she was complaining, he/she said that he/she does not like working with his/her coworker because he/she is rude.
(Action Taken) - I advised the employee that we have a strict policy against employees who are constantly negative about

their work or coworkers. In addition, I told him/her that we take our policies regarding persistent negativity very seriously. If he/she violates this policy in the future, he/she will be subject to discipline, up to and including termination of employment.

(Solution) - The employee will be required to attend a meeting with me within _____ days to discuss this matter. If he/she does not attend this meeting voluntarily, disciplinary action may be taken against him/her, up to and including termination of employment.

Approved By: Date

Manager Signature and Title

115. Unnecessary Workplace Gossip

Workplace gossip is a common occurrence in most workplaces. It is a way for employees to unwind and discuss issues that affect them. However, workplace gossip can cause tension among employees and affect employee performance if it goes overboard. An employee who discusses the personal lives of others during the workday may be using his/her position to obtain personal information about other employees. This is a violation of his/her employer's policy on respect for privacy and misuse of company property, such as the telephone. Use the following template for violation of company policy on unnecessary workplace gossip:

Date

Employee Name

(Problem Relevance) - Violation of Company Policy on Unnecessary Workplace Gossip.

172

(Problem Cause) The cause of the employee's violation is due to the employee's failure to follow a rule.

(Problem Analysis) - On [date], I observed the employee during lunch hour. During this time, he/she was discussing the personal lives of other employees and using our company's telephone during work hours without good reason.

(Action Taken) - I advised the employee that we have a strict policy against employees who discuss the personal lives of other employees or use our company's property for other than its intended purposes. In addition, I told him/her that we take this policy very seriously because it directly affects our productivity and efficiency. If he/she violates this policy in the future, he/she will be subject to discipline, up to and including termination of employment.

(Solution) - The employee will be required to attend a meeting with me within _____ days to discuss this matter. If he/she does not attend this meeting voluntarily, disciplinary action may be taken against him/her, up to and including termination of employment.

Approved By: Date

Manager Signature and Title

116. Personal Hygiene in Workplace

Personal hygiene in the workplace is essential for keeping the workplace clean and safe. Employees who do not maintain their personal hygiene may cause a health hazard in the workplace. In addition, they may offend their coworkers and customers by having a bad odor. As a result, it is important that employees keep themselves clean on duty to prevent any inconvenience in the workplace. Use the following template for violation of company policy on personal hygiene:

Date

Employee Name

(Problem Relevance) - Violation of Company Policy on Personal Hygiene in the Workplace.

(Problem Cause) The cause of the employee's violation is due to his/her failure to follow a rule.

(Problem Analysis) - On [date], I observed the employee _____ in the workplace. When asked why he/she was not clean, he/she said that he/she did not have time to bathe.

(Action Taken) - I advised the employee that we have a strict policy against employees who fail to maintain personal hygiene. In addition, I told him/her that we take our policies regarding personal hygiene very seriously. If he/she violates this policy in the future, he/she will be subject to discipline, up to and including termination of employment.

(Solution) - The employee will be required to attend a meeting with me within _____ days to discuss this matter. If he/she does not attend this meeting voluntarily, disciplinary action may be taken against him/her, up to and including termination of employment.

Approved By: Date

Manager Signature and Title

117. Wrongful Abuse of Authority

Employees may use their workplace authority for their own personal gain by directing or ordering others to do things for them that they should do for themselves. For example, an employee may direct another employee to complete an assignment for him or her, even though the employee who gave the order does not have the authority to do so.

This problem can be difficult to detect and resolve because employees who engage in it often deny they have done anything wrong. Moreover, they often will not admit that they have used their workplace authority for personal gain unless you confront them with specific evidence. They also may attempt to cover up their misdeeds by falsifying documents or destroying incriminating evidence. Once an employee has engaged in this type of misconduct, it is often very important for you to document your actions regarding employees who are suspected or known to engage in it. To help you enforce your policies regarding unauthorized use of workplace authority, use the following template:

Date

Employee Name

(Problem Relevance) - Violation of Company Policy on Unauthorized Use of Authority.

(Problem Cause) - The cause of the violation is ill intention.

(Problem Analysis) - On [date], I observed the employee directing another employee to complete an assignment for him/her. The employee who gave the order did not have the authority to do so.

(Action Taken) -I have advised the employee that he/she is not to direct or order other employees to perform work for him/her unless he/she has been authorized to do so by a supervisor and it is an emergency situation. If he/she does not follow this policy in the future, he/she will be subject to disciplinary action and up to and including termination of employment.

(Solution) The employee will be required to attend a meeting with me within _____ days to discuss this matter. If

he/she does not attend this meeting voluntarily, disciplinary action may be taken against him/her, up to and including termination of employment.

Approved By: Date

Manager Signature and Title

118. Engaging in Improper Political Activity

This section of the employee policy manual should be used to ensure that employees are not engaging in political activity during work hours. This type of activity can not only be disruptive to the workplace, but it can also have a negative impact on productivity. In addition, it may violate policies regarding the level of involvement that your organization allows employees to participate in politics.

Employees who engage in improper political activity are often trying to gain some type of business advantage for themselves or their political candidate by getting the other employees in the organization involved in political activities during work hours. For example, an employee who is involved in improper political activity may try to get his/her coworkers involved by distributing campaign literature or by asking them if they will vote for his/her favorite candidate on Election Day. To ensure that your organization's employees do not engage in improper political activity, use the following template:

Date

Employee Name

(Problem Relevance) - Violation of Company Policy on Political Activity.
(Problem Cause) - The cause of the violation is political influence.

(Problem Analysis) - On [date], I received a report from [source] that the employee had engaged in improper political activities. On [date], I also observed the employee making statements to subordinates that indicated his/her support for a particular political candidate. In addition, on [date], I checked our computer system and found that it contained many inappropriate references to politicians and their policies. In addition, on [date], I reviewed our records and found that they contained many inappropriate references to politicians and their policies.

(Action Taken) - I have advised the employee that he/she will be required to attend a meeting with me within _____ days to discuss this matter.

(Solution) - If he/she does not attend this meeting voluntarily, disciplinary action may be taken against him/her, up to and including termination of employment.

Approved By: Date

Manager Signature and Title

119. Solicitation on Behalf of a Third-Party

Use the following template when documenting your actions regarding employees who attempt to sell products and services to your organization on behalf of a third-party:

Date

Employee Name

(Problem Relevance) - Violation of Company Policy on behalf of Third-Parties.
(Problem Cause) - The cause of the violation is financial gain.

(Problem Analysis) - On [date], I received an email from [source] stating that the employee had attempted to sell my organization some items that he/she had received as gifts from a third-party. I also received a telephone call from [source] stating that the employee had solicited (state action) for _____ (name of third party) without disclosing that he/she was doing so on behalf of this company.

(Action Taken) On [date], I spoke to the employee and informed him/her that he/she was not permitted to solicit on behalf of any third-party without first obtaining my permission. He/she agreed not to do so in the future. However, I have reason to believe that he/she may attempt to violate this policy in the future. Therefore, I have ordered him/her to attend a meeting with me within _____ days to discuss this matter.

(Solution) - If he/she does not attend this meeting voluntarily, disciplinary action may be taken against him/her, up to and including termination of employment.

Approved By: Date

Manager Signature and Title

120. Imposing Political Beliefs on Others

Employees should not impose their political beliefs on others. For example, they should not try to persuade other employees to support a particular candidate for political office or even try to influence their friends and family members to vote for a particular candidate. Employees should also be careful not to use company time or resources for such purposes. In doing so, they can violate company policies on activity during working hours or misuse of company property for those purposes. Use the following template for violation of company policy on imposing political beliefs:

Date

Employee Name

(Problem Relevance) - Violation of Company Policy on Imposing Political Beliefs on Others.

(Problem Cause) The cause of the employee's violation is due to the employee's imposition of his/her political beliefs on others.

(Problem Analysis) - On [date], I observed the employee during working hours talking to other employees about a particular candidate for public office and trying to persuade them to vote for that candidate. In addition, I learned that the employee has been using company property to print out information in favor of a political candidate.

(Action Taken) - I advised the employee that we have a strict policy against employees imposing their political beliefs on others. In addition, I told him/her that we take this policy very seriously because it directly affects our reputation as an unbiased company. If he/she violates this policy in the future, he/she will be subject to discipline, up to and including termination of employment.

(Solution) - The employee will be required to attend a meeting with me within _____ days to discuss this matter. If he/she does not attend this meeting voluntarily, disciplinary action may be taken against him/her, up to and including termination of employment.

Approved By: Date

Manager Signature and Title

Conclusion

We hope that you found this book helpful and informative and that your management of employees will be made easier because of it.

We have covered 120 sample write-ups for employee performance problems. We have covered both oral and written warnings. We have also covered documentation of the corrective actions that you may have taken during the course of a progressive discipline process.

Remember, you should not just use these as presented. You should modify them to fit your organization and its unique policies and procedures.

To be effective, discipline must always be fair and consistent. When employees know what is expected of them and what the consequences are for not meeting expectations, they are more likely to produce good results. Those who do not meet expectations should be given clear guidance about how their performance can improve.

Remember, good employees are worth their weight in gold. Treat your valuable employees with fairness and respect. It is always easier to keep good employees than to replace them.

Once again, we wish you the best of luck in your management and supervision of employees.